942·134  PERRY

This book is due for return on or before the last date shown
above: it may, subject to the book not being reserved by
another reader, be renewed by personal application, post, or
telephone, quoting this date and

D0540858

Chelsea Chicks

Chelsea Chicks

Maria Perry

ANDRE DEUTSCH

First published in Great Britain in 2000 by
André Deutsch Limited
76 Dean Street
London
WIV 5HA
www.vci.co.uk

A catalogue record for this book is available from the British Library

ISBN 0 233 99884 5

Typeset by
Derek Doyle & Associates, Liverpool
Printed in Great Britain by
MPG Books, Bodmin, Cornwall

*For Fiona Macdonald
and in memory of Daphne*

Contents

1
Chelsea Chicks

In their teens they are stunners. Parties are their *raison d'être*. Many become co-dependent with their clothes and neglect GCSEs accordingly, but Chelsea Chicks start life as Chelsea's children – nurtured cradle to grave by Peter Jones. The thirties-built department store towers white and sentinel above Sloane Square, its glass and metal curtain-wall curving over the King's Road, still strikingly modern. From the windows of its Coffee Shop you can look down over the nearest thing London has to a continental piazza. Centre stage a flower-seller shelters his wares under a green umbrella. Opposite, the Royal Court Theatre rises gloriously refurbished, while alongside in the brindled orange and white known as Pont Street Dutch, Oriel, the brasserie which recalls both Paris and Oxford serves Pernod and *café au lait*.

'PJ' as the store is affectionately known prides itself on selling wearable clothes, the kind that blend in on any occasion, but authentic Chelsea Chicks stand out in a crowd. Their dress is eclectic, often startling, frequently copied by country cousins and continually photographed. Foreign fashion editors praise them as quintessentially British which is scarcely surprising. Most absorbed 'style anglais' with their mother's milk and certainly through her credit card.

Their baby clothes may have come from Mothercare, their christening robes were antique lace, but sooner or later the creative ones rebel, buying wacky accessories from the boutiques which litter the Royal Borough from Brompton Cross to the World's End. Their first school uniform, however, was bought from Peter Jones. They were taken there at five to be shrouded in blue blazers a size too big, or Glendower grey cut long for growth. Despite these restrictive beginnings most are loyal shoppers. Even the ones who throw convention to the winds and go pink-haired through Youth and Art, return to PJ for tights and light bulbs and to list Jonelle towels in the Bride's Book. At seventy-five, their faces cherished by Oil of Olay, they still pop in from King's Road wearing mock-croc leggings and thigh-length boots to try out the latest in lip gloss. The truth is: *Chelsea Chicks never grow old.*

They are not to be confused with 'Sloanes', that conformist brigade, who ranged through the eighties and who, in a world ruled by Joseph, remain wilfully accoutred in Hermès and pearls. No, Chelsea Chicks hit headlines. Some are featured by *Vogue* wearing improbable ballgowns, or nothing but their nighties. The ones for whom hair care is a religion get into *Tatler*. Wannabes make the *Sun* and the real extroverts are given a column by the *Sunday Times*. My friend Fiona was once thrown on a mossy bank with her red-gold hair spread out like Ophelia all over *Harpers & Queen*.

A few of Chelsea's children come unstuck, sad cases who take to sampling drugs and practising recreational sex at an unsuitably early age, but Chelsea is a family place, full of remedial practitioners. The day's news begins in Waitrose. It escalates on its way up the King's Road and peaks at tea-time among the leather-topped seats which sprout like toadstools in the Coffee Shop at Peter Jones.

On some mornings Waitrose is like the ante-room of a court for matrimonial causes. If a particular union has gone wrong, the check-out queues are bursting with experts, who can recommend any amount of therapies ranging from acupuncture to marriage guidance. Yogic breathing is nowadays a popular alternative to throwing the dishes, though of course there is always the danger that students will be in too much of a hurry and skip to the chapter on Tantric orgasm before they are ready for it.

The grannies of Cadogan Square are also a solid phalanx of worldly comforters, proof against every disaster. They are a broad-minded lot. Some are pillars of the Anglican Church and will proffer a gin and tonic rather than a handbook on Feng Shui. Others are guardians of great hereditary secrets, such as which public schools have cavities under the floor-boards for concealing cannabis - organically grown, of course. Saving the Planet is big in SW3.

A lot of grannies still live in Old Church Street and serve Earl Grey tea in Spode cups and saucers. They will tell you about the war, when a German bomb hit the Old Church, leaving only the More Chapel standing, but they have usually done something interesting like climbing the Andes in their summer vacations. Some grannies have gone through two or three husbands and accumulated great treasures. Like Grendel's mother in *Beowulf*, they watch over mighty ring hoards, their fingernails gleaming in purple and blue.

The earliest Chelsea Chick of note may well have been a fan of the *Beowulf* poet, whose works were sometimes read aloud amidst a lot of ale-quaffing. She was an Anglo-Saxon Princess, the daughter of King Offa, who unified Mercia and built a dyke to keep out the Welsh. He put Chelsea on the map, just after the Romans left and before the Normans arrived, by building a palace beside the Thames, roughly where Cremorne Road swerves into Cheyne Walk. Offa's daughter was supposed to marry the son of King Charlemagne, but the plans fell through when Offa suggested a French princess should be thrown in as part of the deal. The Franks got very huffy and started a trade war. In 789 AD they closed their ports to the Saxons who, deprived of French wines, cheerfully went back to swilling English beer.

As usual farmers suffered most. The beastly Franks were fighting the equally beastly Huns and there was an outbreak of rinderpest, a European cattle disease. British beef was hit in 810. Charlemagne, whose head was stamped on much of the coinage which reached our shores, was widely blamed. The collective memory runs deep. King Offa's palace now lies buried under the six tower blocks of the World's End Estate. When there is an exceptionally low tide the sturdy piers of his landing stage can be seen poking through the Thames mud. Beer-drinking and a reluctance to embrace the European currency are still strong characteristics of the area.

2
Naughty Antics

A time-honoured jingle reminds us of the matrimonial problems which blighted the life of King Henry VIII, who purchased the Manor of Chelsea in 1536. It runs, 'Divorced, beheaded, died, divorced, beheaded, survived.' The survivor was Katherine Parr, a buxom widow of thirty-something, who came rustling up to court in sumptuous silks with a pack of little greyhounds yapping at her heels in the hot summer of 1543. The greyhounds, it seems, were strokeable, which endeared Lady Latimer as she then was, to the King's younger children, Elizabeth and Edward. The royal libido, which had been under a bit of a cloud, revived accordingly and Henry proposed. 'What a man is the King. How many wives will be marry?' said a tactless maid of honour. She was reprimanded severely.

With a broad grin on his face the King repeated the marriage vows for the sixth time at Hampton Court in the presence of his daughters, the Princesses Mary and Elizabeth, and of his niece and the Bishop of Winchester. The Bishop, who was also Chancellor of Cambridge University, must have sighed with relief to see his sovereign supporting the divine institution of matrimony so fervently and with such an educated lady. Katherine Parr was said by all who knew her to be a paragon of godly learning. The past twelve months had been a trying time for the Bishop: an outbreak of reformist ideals at Cambridge had coincided with civil disobedience in the north and the King's summer holiday had ended in a Royal Sex Scandal of epic proportions.

'The royal libido, which had been under a bit of a cloud, revived accordingly . . .'

Executions had followed when it was confirmed that Henry's fifth consort, Catherine Howard, had committed adultery with her cousin Thomas Culpeper and the pair had been foolish enough to get caught. Instead of accepting the inevitable death sentence with a merry joke, like Sir Thomas More, who died like a gentleman, Catherine Howard had run screaming down a corridor at Hampton Court. Everyone thought it bad form and she was overheard by the future Virgin Queen, the nine-year-old Princess Elizabeth, who clearly became a victim of post traumatic stress. It was affecting her Latin. Worse still, the King of France had written a letter of condolence - a really snide little note, implying that the King of England was no good at choosing wives and that he habitually mixed with persons of 'naughty demeanour'.

When the virtuous and mature Lady Latimer exchanged her widow's weeds for the robes of a Queen of England, therefore, the nation welcomed her with open arms and Parliament set about providing her with a jointure. It included a life interest in Chelsea Manor, a pleasant red-brick house with tall chimneys, a gothic front door and easy access from the river. Henry's other surviving consort, the Lady Anne of Cleves, wept tears of anguish when she heard the news. It was the one piece of real estate she longed to own and she would gladly have swapped it for Richmond Palace.

Manor swapping was one of the vices of the age, especially when substantial provision for widows was included. It put a lot of strain on Chancery, where there was always a backlog of cases from lords and ladies who wanted to exchange parcels of land which they had inherited in inconvenient parts of England. Sir Thomas More was the only person ever known to have cleared Chancery of all the manor-swapping cases and, saint though he was, even he went in for orgies of self-congratulation over the feat. He was sentenced to death in 1535 and canonized four hundred years later. They put up a statue of him on Chelsea Embankment, roughly on the site of his own garden, which stretched from Beaufort Street to the farthest approaches of Cheyne Walk.

'Chelsey', when Sir Thomas settled there was scarcely even a hamlet. A series of water meadows lay along the river bank, which was edged by small sandy beaches, where royal barges could safely berth if their passengers had a sudden whim to go ashore. There was good grazing and More, a successful young lawyer who lived at Bucklersbury in the heart of the City, decided to build a palatial country house with a home farm attached. This meant he could pursue a Utopian lifestyle surrounded by his family and friends, who all made polished Latin jokes while drinking French wines and English organic milk, although I am sorry to say that Sir Thomas was not a believer in free range eggs. In fact, he pioneered an incubation technique, which probably makes him a most unsaintly precursor of battery farming.

He also planted a mulberry grove to encourage the wearing of English silk. Unfortunately he planted the wrong sort of mulberry trees. Silkworms spin best after gorging on *morus alba* the leaves of the white mulberry tree, but Sir Thomas, who could never resist a good pun, planted *morus nigra*, a play on the word 'blackamoor'. The joke misfired, as the silkworms didn't like the leaves, so he gave the plantation to his daughter Margaret when she married William Roper, throwing in an orchard for good measure. Roper's orchard still survives as a place name at the bottom of Danvers Street. A little further along the Embankment if you peer discreetly into the hallway of 90 Cheyne Walk, there is a beautiful modern mural, showing what More's house looked like in its heyday.

While the builders were at work, More and his family lived in the old farm house, where the western part of Cheyne Walk now looks out over the river. When the main rooms were complete, Sir Thomas moved in adding a chapel, a library and a fine garden in the Italian style, where as Lord Chancellor of England, he could stroll about with the King as they discussed affairs of state. Mostly they talked about foreign policy, but one day the King put his arm around More's shoulders, which prompted Sir Thomas to remark prophetically that if Henry thought it would gain him one French castle, he would cut off his head.

Shortly after making this ill-timed joke, More was executed, but Henry soon missed the convivial atmosphere of Chelsea, so he bought up the other large house there, which happened to be Chelsea Manor whose river frontage extended the whole length of what is today the eastern part of Cheyne Walk. Henry immediately improved the gardens by planting a cherry orchard. Eight years later he handed it over to Catherine Parr, who was a seasoned but somewhat extravagant gardener. She ordered lavender bushes and damask roses by the hundred, so that by the 1540 Chelsea's reputation for aromatherapy and high-class horticulture was well under way.

The Queen had little time to do up the house however. Henry had worked himself into one of his rages against the French, who had invaded the Isle of Wight. By way of reprisal, he besieged Boulogne, leaving Catherine as Regent of England. Despite a busy schedule she was the best stepmother the royal children ever had. She sent Henry fortnightly bulletins about their health and, as an early protest against French farming methods, haunches of venison, organically reared at Hampton Court.

When the King died, Catherine moved to Chelsea, taking her thirteen-year-old stepdaughter Princess Elizabeth with her. Everyone approved the arrangement, for it was obvious that in the household of a Dowager Queen who was famed for her piety and learning, Elizabeth would get on with her Latin. No one was prepared for what happened next. Having suffered three husbands, all older than herself, Catherine Parr fell head over heels in love with the Lord Protector's brother, Tom Seymour, Lord High Admiral of England. The Admiral was the boy king's favourite uncle, but the Lord Protector took a dim view of his sibling's alliance with the richest and most powerful lady in the land. The couple exchanged scorching love letters and Catherine admitted that she had loved the Admiral even before she had been proposed to by Henry VIII.

It was the stuff of a novel by Dame Barbara Cartland. Seymour took to rowing down the Thames at dead of night to keep clandestine trysts with the Queen among her damask roses. The whole thing was very bad for Elizabeth's Latin and the Admiral bribed the King with extra pocket-money to sanction his liaison. Very soon the couple were married with royal consent. 'The Lord Seymour of Sudeley maried the Quene, whose nam was Katerine,' wrote the nine-year-old monarch in his diary, adding with evident satisfaction, 'with wich mariag the Lord Protectour was much offended.'

Catherine quickly became pregnant and Tom Seymour, whose erotic instincts were not easily held in check, took to romping half-clad with the maids of honour. It was again bad for Elizabeth's Latin but the Admiral, being a terrible tease, began visiting her early in the mornings in his dressing gown and slippers, though apparently minus the trunk hose which Tudor gentlemen relied upon to disguise their predatory intentions. Sensing another Royal Sex Scandal in the air, Catherine accompanied him one morning as chaperone. Together they tickled the Princess, who retreated behind her bed curtains. Just as the Queen had convinced herself that nothing improper was going on, Mistress Ashley, Elizabeth's lady governess, reported that the Admiral had been caught bottom-smacking. Once again the Queen decided to join her husband in the frolics. She probably thought it was the easiest way to keep an eye on him, but this time the naughty antics went too far.

In an extraordinary episode of sex, or sadism, the Queen held Elizabeth down, while the Admiral cut the girl's dress to ribbons with his sword point. Whether he did it as some form of punishment, or for a wager, or, as one historian suggests, 'To get a sight of her underclothes', it was an incredibly dangerous way to treat the King's younger sister, who happened to be the Protestant heiress to the throne. For the Queen Dowager to act as accomplice suggests incurable voyeurism, or that the pair were drunk and disorderly.

Naturally, the spectacle of a royal princess with her petticoats showing through a slashed kirtle, provoked comment, but it was not until she actually found her stepdaughter in the Admiral's embrace that Catherine lost her cool. Elizabeth was banished to Cheshunt, while the Lord Protector set up an inquiry, detaining the Princess's servants in the Tower of London. Very soon the whole bizarre story was rhymed and jangled in every tavern and ale-house in the town. The Admiral lost his head, which the King cheerfully reported in his diary as another bit of English history. Elizabeth added Greek to her Latin and Chelsea's reputation as a playground for rich eccentrics had begun.

3
The King's Road

The spirit of playful adventure which Catherine and her Admiral brought to the banks of the Thames went into abeyance during the Commonwealth, that dour period of English history, when Cromwell and his Roundheads held sway. At the accession of Charles II, however, things brightened up. The Merry Monarch was swift to sample the rustic pleasures of Chelsea. He arrived at Dover on 25 May 1660 with soldiers, courtiers, diplomats, his brothers Prince James and Prince Henry and the indefatigable diarist, Samuel Pepys, in tow. To set the well-known tone of Restoration England, his mistress Barbara Villiers, who was married to the complaisant Cavalier Roger Palmer, was also of the party. She was soon to be made Lady Castlemaine and ultimately, Duchess of Cleveland. Barbara contrived to upset the Queen by giving birth to five of Charles's bastards.

Shortly after his coronation the King discovered a bathing place on the sandy stretches of the Thames between Westminster and Putney. He improved the muddy farm track, which ran through the fields not far from the present Embankment and appropriated it to his own use. It became known as 'the King's private road' and what had previously been a well-trodden lane, used by farmers and gardeners taking produce to the City of London, was gravelled to take a horse-drawn carriage. Instead of using the river, which was the normal route between the Palace of Westminster and Hampton Court, the King could travel at reasonable speed as far as Putney

Bridge and then embark for the last stage of his journey into Surrey. King's Road stories and Merry Monarch lore soon abounded. Chelsea is a great place for the telling of tales, and in the telling and the retelling, fact and romantic fiction mingle convincingly. Dates also get shifted about with remarkable abandon. Take Founder's Day at the Royal Hospital as a case in point.

The mellow red-brick building which hosts the annual Flower Show in its spacious grounds was set up in 1682. King Charles wished it to rival les Invalides in France and no expense was spared. Sir Christopher Wren designed the accommodation around three elegant courtyards and the story goes that when Nell Gwyn, the most practical of the King's mistresses, saw the plans, she tore her handkerchief into strips and laid them out to show that the central quadrangle needed to be twice the size. In some versions of her c.v. Nell's father was a soldier, so she was familiar with the proportions of a parade ground. Be that as it may, Charles laid the foundation stone of the new building with his own hand in a terrific ceremony attended by half the nobility and gentry of England.

Founder's Day was celebrated on 29 May, the King's birthday, also known as Oak Apple Day in commemoration of his miraculous escape after the Battle of Worcester, which was fought in the first week of September. There are several accounts, but all concur that a party of Cromwell's men were searching Boscombe Wood for surviving Cavaliers, while above their heads, heavily disguised as a wood-cutter in a green coat and ill-fitting shoes, the fugitive monarch was hiding up an oak tree. The King told the story himself – many times – after the Restoration and Pepys set it down when an authorized version was agreed.

In due course Founder's Day at the Royal Hospital was changed because the last week in May fell too close to another anniversary of national import, the birthday of King George III on 4 June. It is hard to understand why the dates were thought to clash but, as Queen Charlotte always threw lavish parties for her husband, including magic lanterns and royal fireworks, it must be supposed that the authorities did not wish to give the Chelsea Pensioners cause to get drunk twice in one week. In the 1920s when the Flower Show became an annual fixture, Founder's Day had to be changed again. The first Thursday in June was substituted and on this day pensioners in their red coats and tricorne hats parade to honour the memory of King Charles. They also drink the health of Nell Gwyn.

According to a few killjoy historians, led by the diarist John Evelyn, 'pretty, witty Nell' had nothing to do with the founding of the hospital. Evelyn insists that the true originator of the scheme was Sir Stephen Fox, who put up the money to buy the site, for the Hospital was built on land which at that time belonged to the Royal Society. A more romantic tradition insists that on one occasion when the King's mistress was driving in her coach, she was stopped by a one-legged soldier who had been wounded by the Moors at the siege of Tangier and had then had his leg shot off by a Dutch privateer. Filled with compassion, she went to her royal lover and entreated him to build almshouses where old soldiers could end their days in comfort and under proper supervision. Pepys supported the scheme and, as a token of gratitude, Nell gave him an engraving of herself as Cupid wearing only a pair of wings. He hung it in his office at the Admiralty, an early version of the Pirelli calendar.

Nell herself is thought to have had a house at Strand's End, which lay just over the parish border in Fulham, near the present-day Lot's Road. Her feelings about care for the elderly may have been influenced by the fact that her mother had died at Chelsea three years earlier. The old lady had fallen dead drunk into a ditch at Sandy End, the stream which divided the parishes. The newspaper reports implied that Mrs Gwyn was so fat and heavy that rescuers could not lift her out in time to save her. Nell gave her mother a magnificent funeral at St Martin-in-the-Fields. Heraldic devices were drawn up for the coffin and the Earl of Rochester rose poetically to the occasion with:

Five gilded scutcheons did the hearse enrich,
To celebrate this martyr of the Ditch.

The old lady's favourite tipple was brandy which was burned in flaming sconces at the funeral and drunk in prodigious quantities to honour the deceased matron. She was reputed to get through several quarts a day and a number of the London brandy merchants attended the obsequies. Various comic epitaphs of the time suggest that Mrs Gwyn lived in a cow-shed; certainly Sandy End was the most rustic part of Chelsea and the lifestyle of its inhabitants was very different from that of the Cheyne family who, just before the Restoration, had purchased Katherine Parr's old manor house at the grander end of the waterfront.

By the time Charles had resurfaced, the King's Road, Chelsea was becoming what Daniel Defoe was later to call 'a Town of Palaces'. Shrewder members of the English nobility had recognized the amenities, beloved by More and Henry VIII. They began to build large country houses there, or to adapt and refurbish existing properties. Just before the sale of the Old Manor House to Charles Cheyne on the eve of the Restoration, a previous occupant the Marquis of Hamilton, had added an extension. This was eventually to be known as Winchester House, as it was acquired by the Bishops of Winchester. One of their number, Bishop Ken, was a dreadful old prude who refused accommodation to Nell Gwyn, when the court went to Winchester, which the King proposed to turn into a centre for autumnal field sports. The Bishop was not remotely interested in banning hunting, but he was completely out of sympathy with the progressive Restoration ethic, which encouraged the Supreme Head of the Church of England to believe he should lodge a royal whore beneath an episcopal roof. 'A woman of ill repute', he pointed out, 'ought not to be endured in the house of a clergyman, least of all that of the King's chaplain.' Charles, whose first tutor had been the Bishop of Chichester, treated him with respect.

The same spirit of gentlemanly discretion must have been what prompted him to commandeer the King's Road for his private use. Deserted fields lay on either side and the rural vista was broken only by a few pieces of monumental masonry, such as the gates to the Duke of Beaufort's private driveway, which stood approximately on the site of the present Beaufort Street traffic lights. Nell's house, later dignified by the Victorians with the name of Sandford Manor, lay further along the route. Opinions differ about its décor. One worried topographer was to lament that 'walnut trees perhaps planted by a royal hand' had been viciously uprooted to make way for the gasworks. The Victorians pictured Nell as a frail woman lured by the wickedness of the age. The theory cannot have been shared by Sir Peter Lely, for whom she posed unselfconsciously naked, as a delicious Venus, with the Duke of St Albans, her bastard son by the King, kneeling like a sturdy Cupid at her side.

We must picture Charles, therefore, one peaceful afternoon speeding along his private road towards Nell Gwyn's premises in Fulham. His goal was rest and recreation, and that part of his anatomy which Nell and the Earl of Rochester had christened his 'big engine' was perhaps softly stirring beneath the baggy satin breeches which etiquette and French fashion pundits had decreed proper attire for Kings of England and their courtiers. Suddenly, in the stretch between the Duke of Beaufort's gateway and the site of the present Slaidburn Street, the royal carriage lurched to a halt. The postilion leaped down, as though struck by lightning. An axle had broken. It was circa 1668 and there was no hope of calling the AA.

Languid and gentlemanly, King Charles descended onto the newly gravelled surface. He surveyed the muddy fields which stretched to the horizon on his right and the sand banks on his left. Drawing on his picturesque store of oaths, he cried 'Odd's blood, it would have to happen at the World's End.' Thus, they say, did the area between the Beaufort Street traffic lights and the present World's End public house gain its name. At other hostelries in the area an alternative tradition persists. Go into the Man in the Moon, or the Water Rat and they will assure you that the mud and the sand dunes are a myth. A low dive stood beside the King's Road. When the axle broke Charles took shelter and called for ale. He had never before tasted such beastly beer and cursed the place and all who served in it.

4
Something in the Air

In Queen Anne's reign the King's Road became 'the Queen's private road'. It was still used by local people to carry fruit, flowers and farm-produce to London. Nurseries and market gardens began to replace some of the open fields, but the idea that the road should be reserved for the monarch's private use appealed greatly to George I. In 1719 there was a proposal to withdraw the right of way. A few houses had been built along the roadside, so there was an immediate hullabaloo. By this time the Cheyne family, having perpetuated their name in the riverside walk, had sold the Old Manor House to Sir Hans Sloane. He was Secretary of the Royal Society and not a man to be trifled with. As Lord of the Manor, he joined Dr King the Rector of Chelsea, to protest against the closure. After some legal squabbling with the Royal Household the ancient right of way was preserved, to the annoyance of the King, who was finding English local government a good deal tougher than commanding the Imperial Army on the Rhine. Passes were issued in the form of lead and copper tokens stamped 'the King's Private Road' on one side and with the royal monogram on the other. Tollgates were set up and King George, who had just lost £100,000 in the South Sea Bubble, must have appreciated the income.

The King's Road ceased to be a private thoroughfare in 1830. It has been in a continuing frenzy of redevelopment ever since. Market gardens gave way to residential squares, where trade was not permitted and the only building tolerated, other than private houses, was a church, but the road itself became crammed with small shops and markets. Scornful residents, who remembered the area when it was more sedate, dubbed it 'Chelsea High Street' and the commercial life of the village, which had first sprung up near the waterside, gradually refocused around the road. Yet despite the snobberies of the Victorian age, which so emphasized the gulf between Society and Trade, the area never went downmarket.

When Thomas Crapper the sanitary engineer opened premises there in 1907, he was the holder of three Royal Warrants; Edward VII's mistress, Lillie Langtry, had ordered a special armchair in blue velvet to fit over her water closet when the King called. Even among the tradesmen an exotic and fashionable milieu predominated. There was, as Mary Quant was to remark some fifty years lager, 'something in the air' which drew eccentric, flamboyant, but eminently *stylish* people to live and work in the King's Road. The Pheasantry, which in the 1860s used to sell pheasants for breeding stock, had its present triumphal arch added in the 1880s by the Joubert family. They were French cabinet-makers, who saw fit to announce their presence with an exuberant parody of the Arc du Carousel. The current owners, Pizza Express, have wisely preserved its glories. High above the road, a bronze charioteer reins in four prancing steeds who seem poised to gallop off into the Marks & Spencer car park which stands opposite. Two caryatids flank the arch and on the gateposts two bronze eagles prepare to swoop on passing pedestrians. M. Joubert was an armourer as well as a cabinet-maker and in the course of time, created tournament armour for the miniature figures in Queen Mary's dolls' houses.

After 1914 the building was made into studios. Two years later Princess Astafieva, the beautiful Russian ballet-dancer, taught there. She came to London with Diaghilev and danced before George V and Queen Mary when the Ballet Russe performed for them before the Coronation. Astafieva's star pupils included Alicia Markova, Anton Dolin and Margot Fonteyn. When Diaghilev returned to London after the Russian Revolution, he brought Nijinsky with him and the great dancer used to perform for the nurses in St Stephen's Hospital, showering them with golden roubles. Astafieva displayed the same generosity: at the end of a class she would say majestically, 'Those who *can* – pay.' Later the Pheasantry became a club for intelligent Bohemians. Annigoni, Francis Bacon, the ubiquitous Lucian Freud and Augustus John were habitués and, beating the floor with his crutches, Robert Newton, the hard-drinking actor who played Long John Silver in *Treasure Island.*

While Astafieva taught classical dance a new craze had broken out among the privileged classes. Further down the King's Road, beside the Vale, the Blue Bird Garage provided all the services required by those who had grown addicted to motoring. It was the largest garage in Europe with space for 300 cars. Bright young things in goggles, their cloche hats secured by voluminous scarves or held in place by the latest patent fasteners, roared up to refuel Lagondas, or to have their tyres inflated at one of the sixty pneumatic air-pumps. There were waiting rooms and writing rooms for ladies, owner-drivers and chauffeurs. Donald Campbell, holder of the world land-speed record, named all his racing cars 'Bluebird' after the garage and when Sir Terence Conran converted it into the present gastrodome, he retained bluebirds on the gateposts. But it was the fashion explosion of the 1960s which really put the King's Road on the map.

'I love London,' said Diana Vreeland, the editor of American *Vogue.* 'It is a swinging City.' Suddenly the King's Road became the epicentre of all that was new and wild, and cool in the fashion world. Boutiques ousted the department store. The colours were psychedelic; the names echoed the drug culture. 'Granny Takes a Trip' and 'I was Lord Kitchener's Valet' were packed on Saturday mornings with the new élite – pop stars, models, Twiggy look-alikes and suburban teenagers hoping they would be picked up by David Bailey. The girls flicked back manes of long, clean, shining hair in imitation of Jean Shrimpton, who had become the most famous cover-girl ever. The men wore lace-ruffled shirts which would not have disgraced Charles II's cavaliers. Reigning supreme was Mary Quant, who launched the miniskirt from a bedsitter in Oakley Street. Her first shop was

Bazaar on the corner of Markham Square, *the* place to be seen on a sunny Saturday afternoon. For this was Chelsea; this was Celebrityville.

Mary Quant was firmly in the forefront of the great sixties happening. She and her teenage sweetheart, Alexander Plunket Greene had met at art school and they bought the freehold of tumbledown Markham House with money which was part of his twenty-first present. The Chelsea Society objected. 'Put the house back as it was,' they howled as raffish mannequins in striped bathing costumes, or the skirts known later as 'bum frills' stared across the King's Road, almost opposite Chelsea's Georgian gem, Wellington Square. Every day the shop would sell out of stock and Mary used to rush into Harrods to buy more fabric, which was stitched up at Oakley Street overnight.

In the basement young Plunket Greene started Alexander's, the restaurant patronized by the whole of Swinging London. Mary once described it as 'like a permanent cocktail party'. On the first floor, Bazaar was packed with the avant-garde young buying miniskirts and black tights, which had suddenly become the hallmark of the Chelsea girl. They were thought to be daring and rather louche. Downstairs, Italian waiters served the seven-and-sixpenny set lunch. Alexander's aunts, who had vaguely ducal connections, visited the restaurant as, on one occasion, did Prince Rainier and Princess Grace of Monaco, accompanied by detectives with pistols bulging under their armpits. On another occasion, the waiters stood open-mouthed as Brigitte Bardot arrived with a posse of press and paparazzi. Bardot, thinking they were impressed by her, smiled ever more sweetly at the cameras, but the waiters had been swept off their feet by the ravishing young Adonis the star had in tow. Sixties camp had set in.

Upstairs at Bazaar the tiny dressing-rooms could present problems but when film-star Kay Kendall arrived with her six pugs and in a terrible hurry, Alexander rose heroically to the occasion. Scooping up the dresses the great actress wished to try on, he led her down to the restaurant, which was, fortunately, empty at the time. She promptly unzipped the dress she was wearing and the Plunket Greene hormones went into overdrive when he saw that she was quite naked underneath. She bought four dresses. As London swung, the pop scene and the fashion world became inextricably mingled. The Beatles had arrived from Liverpool with a vibrant new rock sound. They were followed by the Rolling Stones. Ossie Clark came from Manchester – it was the first time the Royal College of Art had seen a male student in pink gingham shorts – and the moment he graduated he was dressing Beatle wives. The scene expanded to Notting Hill, but it was still Chelsea that was known for the most daring parties. Mick Jagger brought a pelvic thrust to British pop, the like of which had not been seen since Elvis rocked America. He explored the wilder shores of love with Marianne Faithfull, the blonde who looked like the girl next door and was married to John Dunbar.

In 1967 Jonathan King sang 'Everyone's Gone to the Moon'. Shortly afterwards Stanley Kubrick's science-fiction movie *2001, A Space Odyssey* was playing in the Chelsea Classic and filmgoers gasped at the special effects as the hostess retrieved a floating fountain pen which defied gravity, deftly replacing it in the pocket of a sleeping passenger. A year later it was for real: Man reached the Moon. In Paris, Courrèges launched Moon boots. Ungaro cut triangular clothes. In London, Vidal Sassoon cut triangular fringes. Quant was declared Woman of the Year. She married Alexander and it was whispered in the Kenco Coffee Bar that she had shaved her pubic hair into the shape of a perfect heart.

5
Chelsea is an Attitude of Mind

The oldest rendering of Chelsea is in a document written in Saxon times, where it appears as 'Cealchylle'. This outlandish spelling upset the Normans, who styled it 'Cercehede' and 'Chelched'. Both versions occur in the Domesday Book, but they clearly refer to the same place. At some point in the Middle Ages, a scribe with a lisp wrote it 'Chelcheth', which someone with posh enunciation, perhaps a Lady Abbess, corrupted to 'Chelchith'. This became standard upper-class usage, but it endangered the hearer with a shower of spittle, particularly if uttered by a careless peasant, and so gave way to the more modish 'Chelsey' as the sixteenth century dawned. Etymologists over the years have had a wonderful time tracing the name back to the 'chesel' or mixture of sand and pebbles, which was found along the foreshore.

This name is delightfully echoed in Chesil Court, a 1930s block of startling modernity when it was first built. It is cream and curvaceous with Art Nouveau front doors and gleaming chrome light switches. Its most venerable inhabitant is Lord Longford, who was once an Oxford don, twice Lord Privy Seal and, for a brief spell, First Lord of the Admiralty. He is now a Prison Visitor and a national institution. My friend Nigel used to live there too. He bought wine at auction and his sofa was always draped with Chelsea Chicks with enormously long legs, sniffing at priceless Tokay. They had come to admire the pictures. Close friends were invited to inspect Nigel's bathroom. I, who have no taste in pictures, still lust after 'Bluebells in a Wood', which hung directly above the wash basin. Towards the end of his tenure the bathroom walls required repairs revealing, to everyone's astonishment, that Chesil Court really did seem to be built of sand and pebbles.

At Oxford Nigel was a dashing young lawyer, who looked and dressed like a character from Noël Coward. He wore a carnation and could reduce a cocktail party to tears of helpless laughter simply by saying that he came from 'Chelseah'. He would imbue the whole of the last syllable with an air of aristocratic bohemianism. He is a mainstay of the Chelsea Society and masterminds its annual exhibitions with taste and erudition. Everyone loves Nigel and everyone agrees that the Chelsea Society could not do without him, for it is a part of Nigel's charm to be indispensable. Sometimes, however, he gets carried away by his enthusiasm for architectural detail and on such mornings Waitrose is filled with furtive shoppers, skulking behind Household Detergents, or poring intently over Organic Meat. They are avoiding Nigel. On days when he is fully charged, a sort of radar alert goes round, because people know that if they stop to say 'Hello Nigel', they will get caught up in whatever topic is preying on his mind.

It was particularly difficult the year the Chelsea Society featured Inigo Jones in their annual exhibition. One Chelsea Chick scurrying to avoid a dissertation on how the Inigo Jones gateway was moved to Chiswick House because she was shopping conscientiously for a dinner party, ducked behind Breakfast Cereals and fell straight upon the manly breast of the Indian Brave. He was a genuine Cherokee and shopped daily in Waitrose, wearing his native headdress, moccasins and leather trousers. He went bare-chested even in December. Fiona once manoeuvred herself behind him in the check-out queue to peer into his trolley. It was full of Honey Puffs.

You don't get that eclectic social mix in Selfridges' Wine and Food Department, which is probably what makes Waitrose in the King's Road, or a browse round Sir Terence Conran's Gastrodome, seem such an adventure. It was jolly rude of Fiona to stare into the Indian Brave's trolley, especially when she'd been sent to Saturday morning classes in the school holidays to

. . . and fell straight upon the manly breast of the Indian Brave.

learn ballroom dancing and curtseying from Susan Hampshire's mother. I reckon it's exactly that wild kind of social permissiveness, though, which led Nigel to say 'Chelsea is an attitude of mind.'

We all thought he was terribly clever. As an identifiable location, after all, the place is a mass of contradictions. Even select members of the Chelsea Society cannot agree its boundaries. Some insist that 'the Egertons' - that network of confusingly named Gardens, Terraces and Crescents south of Brompton Road – are Chelsea on the grounds that the post code is SW3. Others hold steadfastly that they are ethnically and geographically Knightsbridge. It is a great worry for American visitors, who check in to the Franklin Hotel expecting it to be Bohemian. Having heard that Chelsea is 'London's Left Bank', they arrive direct from California with colourfully casual wardrobes to find that the décor is pure SW1 and that the bedrooms have been imposingly done up by a Scottish duchess. Even stalwart Republicans feel they should have packed something to change into for dinner.

A further hazard is the development of Brompton Cross, where the new ethos confuses even the natives. A few years ago it was a comforting outpost of the 1950s, full of small shops where you could buy anything from newspapers to pipe-cleaners. Then Joseph opened a little emporium selling simple leather jackets. He expanded to become one of the grandest names in European prêt-à-porter and now owns most of Draycott Avenue. The problem for the locals is that not everyone wishes to be stamped by the hallmark of global chic, while popping out to buy milk or the *Evening Standard*. In the old days, but within living memory, Joe the Milkman delivered the milk by horse and cart. After Joe acquired an electric milk float, many people remember hearing him say 'Gee-up' from sheer force of habit, as he slipped off the hand-brake. When the Michelin building turned into Bibendum, selling oysters and bouquets in waxed paper, some folk felt it was the last straw. 'You used to be able to walk down the street in pyjamas and nobody would turn a hair,' remembers Judy Yeatman-Biggs.

'Now the place is so up-market you can only go out in designer pyjamas.'

A good rule of thumb for working out where Knightsbridge ends and Chelsea begins would seem to be to study the parish boundaries. They have been drawn up with skill and intricacy and you can pore over them by appointment in the parish office of St Luke-and-Christchurch on weekday mornings. St Luke's broods with cathedral-like intensity over Sydney Street, having replaced Chelsea Old Church, where Sir Thomas More worshipped, as parish church. It was dedicated to St Luke who is the official patron of the area.

He has been eclipsed by St Thomas More. By the beginning of the nineteenth century Chelsea's population had increased dramatically. On Sunday mornings the faithful could no longer fit into the Old Church. Artisans and agricultural labourers were wedged next to the nobility and gentry. The aroma was indescribable. Something bigger was needed. By 1824 James Savage had completed St Luke's. Its tower is the highest in Chelsea and its flying buttresses are a gem of Gothic Revival, but the area is divided into *twelve* smaller parishes. Even to high dignitaries of the Anglican Church the boundaries are an esoteric mystery. They zigzag erratically across the map from Redcliffe Gardens (geographically Earl's Court but spiritually Chelsea) to Holy Trinity Sloane Square, which teeters on the borders of Belgravia. Holy Trinity, the temple of the Arts and Crafts Movement, was faced with closure until they drafted in the Very Reverend Michael Marshall, the Assistant Bishop of London, to save it. An energetic socializer and a talented pianist, the Bishop has style. He administers Holy Communion in a golden mitre and gives sherry parties at the Basil Street Hotel, but is not to be confused with the Reverend Sandy Miller, the Vicar of Holy Trinity, Brompton.

As well as the two Holy Trinities, there are *two* St Lukes and two Christchurches in Chelsea. On the map, one of the Christ Church boundaries ricochets through the heart of Knightsbridge, slicing across Cadogan Square to stop short of the tube station. The postal districts then cut willy-nilly through the parishes. At the 'Gasworks End', intensely fashionable ever since Prince William danced at Crazy Larry's, the Cremorne Estate and Lot's Road are SW10. Diana pilgrims in search of the Harbour Club, where the late Princess went for her workouts, are deeply puzzled to find Chelsea Harbour is Hammersmith and Fulham, a reality the new international set finds hard to take, especially if they have just forked out several million pounds for a penthouse overlooking Battersea Reach. They are campaigning strenuously to be SW3. Needless to say, Chelsea Football Club is in Fulham.

Foreigners are always astonished by the geographical extent of the Royal Borough of Kensington and Chelsea. It runs from the river in the south to the furthest confines of Kensal Green Cemetery in the north. Its inhabitants are racially integrated, but their cultural values differ from those the Prime Minister is trying to instil into the nation at large. The Conservative Club is at the World's End. It sells the cheapest beer in London and its membership is predominantly working class. If you ask about politics in 'the Rileys', the 'village pub' of the tower blocks, the response will be a big grin and 'We're all Conservatives here.'

At one time Kensington and Chelsea had separate town halls and two Lord Mayors. The boroughs were merged in 1964 for administrative reasons. There was a lot of tut-tutting. Her Majesty the Queen had to issue letters patent extending the prefix 'Royal' to Chelsea. Quite a few sticklers for convention thought no good would come of it. Queen Victoria had created Kensington a 'Royal' borough in 1901 'to confer a distinction on her own birthplace', and even in the swinging sixties, the sedate residents of De Vere Gardens did not care to be associated with the louche goings-on at the Chelsea Arts Club, or to be lumped in with the wilder element at Manresa Road. Not even the fact that the last Mayor of Chelsea was the seventh Earl Cadogan mitigated the stigma.

Shortly after the boroughs merged, Kensington Town Hall became the political nerve centre and conservationists immediately complained because the building was modern, not Gothic Revival. Chelsea Town Hall, meanwhile, with its imposing pillared façade, became 'the Old Town Hall', housing a library, a register office and Social Services, which are tucked away round the back. Kensington's unemployed are sent to 'sign on' in Hammersmith.

The swimming baths on the Chelsea Manor Street side of the 'Old Town Hall' have recently became the Chelsea Sports Centre. It is immensely flash and at one point began to compete with the Harbour Club in the number of its facilities, although the patrons are from a different income group and there was wailing and gnashing of teeth when the admission charges went up. For a time a delicious sauna operated, but it had to be closed down when unmarried couples were discovered using it for unauthorized sex.

At the back of the Town Hall an extension was added in the 1880s which is now used as exhibition space. An Antiques Fair is held there in the spring and a prestigious Craft Fair in the autumn. Sandwiched between the two comes the Chelsea Festival, when the Chelsea Society puts on its annual presentation. Waitrose throbs with vibrantly clad Chelsea Chicks, who compete to assist Nigel with the preparations. Banners advertise all principal events giving the impression that the stretch of King's Road between Heal's and the Fire Station is permanently en fête.

Furniture for the Antiques Fair, woolly mittens for the Craft Fair and wondrous displays by the Chelsea Society, explaining where drinking chocolate could be bought in the eighteenth century, all have to be carried in and out of the old Town Hall. This means that traffic is regularly brought to a standstill by illegally parked pantechnicons. Wardens in the RBKC's smart blue uniforms travel in posses; they are verbally abused by owner-drivers of all races and denominations.

In between these annual fixtures the Town Hall has become a favourite venue for Psychic Events. There are fairs to promote gemology, reflexology, Tarot readings and Tibetan reiki. You can buy crystals and rare incense. You can have your aura photographed and go on Shamanic journeys. Dr Kurtagic, who is a graduate of the Sorbonne and widely regarded by young film-makers as the Sibyl of Oakley Street, was once told her totemic animal was a fish. She bought a goldfish and named him Victor. He is supposed to even out her chakras.

Mind and Spirit Fairs always bring their own devotees and at intervals the King's Road becomes again a rainbow of floating dresses and purple perpendicular hairstyles. The 1970s are reinvoked and Steinberg and Tolkein do a roaring trade in nostalgic bric-à-brac. It is a different ethos altogether from Kensington, where the Duchess of Gloucester opens the Christmas Charity Bazaar and the diplomatic demi-monde buy cut-price pashminas.

6
Great Gardeners

As we have pointed out, when he wasn't beating up the French, or indulging in bouts of domestic violence, Henry VIII was a great gardener. One of his first additions to Chelsea Manor was a cherry orchard, to which the green-fingered Katherine Parr added lavender walks and her famous damask roses. At one point Henry employed a staff of twenty-nine gardeners and six women weeders to plant whitehorn and privet hedges, cherry trees, damson trees, red peach trees and filberts. Filberts are hazelnuts, so it is easy to see why the Royal Household enjoyed Chelsea Manor, with its plentiful supply of homegrown desserts and organic roughage. The first gardener came from Westminster. His name was Henry Russell and he laid the foundations for what became known for the next two hundred years as 'the Great Garden'. The King and Russell probably took the credit although, of course, it was the women weeders who did all the work.

Next door Sir Thomas More's old house was granted to the Marquis of Winchester, although it was coveted by Henry's brother-in-law, the Duke of Suffolk. It went eventually to Queen Elizabeth's chief secretary, Lord Burghley, and the Virgin Queen often visited the house. On one occasion, as she rode across the fields to Chelsea Manor instead of taking the river route, a sudden shower of rain caused her to take shelter under an elm tree. The tree was mentioned in parish registers for decades and its site was marked until recently by the pub at the corner of Fulham Road and Old Church Street, known as the Queen's Elm.

More's house stood some six hundred feet back from the river with grounds extending down to a private water gate with a substantial landing place. He planted an orchard, a mulberry grove and a splendid flower garden, from which his wife, Dame Alice, gathered blooms to decorate the house. Dame Alice had a high sense of style and a sharp, no-nonsense wit. When More became Chancellor of England, if she caught him putting on airs, she would intervene with a swift 'Tilly-valley *Master* More'. As soon as the Chelsea house was built she had to put up with intolerable guests like the Great Erasmus, who was always complaining about English beer. She was also the butt of excruciating jokes from Henry VIII's Latin secretary Ammonio, who said she had a long nose. Lady More stood on her dignity. When Holbein, a friend of the Great Erasmus, painted Sir Thomas and his family, she added her own little status symbols to the scene.

Holbein put in two dogs, three vases filled with flowers and Lady More's pet monkey. The flower vases are crammed with lilies, carnations, columbine, purple iris, honeysuckle and heartsease, and I am prepared to swear (even though it may invite E-mail from outraged horticulturists) one large red tulip. The tulip in the earliest version of the portrait is in a bronze vase directly above Dame Alice's head. It is a lovely scarlet tulip, echoing the tones of her red velvet sleeves and its petals are wide open, because someone who knew damn all about tulips has put it on a window sill in direct sunlight.

Holbein's picture was finished in 1526, but the first tulip is not supposed to have been sighted in Europe until 1559, when one reached Augsburg. That of course was the first *recorded* tulip, so that what this unofficial bloom suggests is that Lady More was a terrific trend-setter in the gardening world. She was fifty-seven at the time of Holbein's portrait and a highly successful stepmother to More's children by his first marriage. She ran a home farm, supervised a vegetable garden and kept up with all the latest fashions. Pet monkeys were the sensation of the season in 1526. The Queen – at that time Katherine of Aragon – had posed for the trendy Flemish miniaturist, Lucus

Hornebolte, in a gown furred with ermine, a monkey noncha-lantly perched on her sleeves. Being a monkey-owner conferred cachet at court. Dame Alice may have had a long nose, but she knew how to choose her accessories.

Art historians have a deep prejudice against monkeys. In Renaissance portraiture they are supposed to symbolize the difference between what Dorothy Parker would have summa-rized as the deep peace of the marriage bed and the hurly-burly of the chaise longue. Chained monkeys stood for discreet procreative sex. Unchained ones meant something darker. The whole court supported procreative sex in 1526, as England still lacked a male heir to the throne. Eminent gynaecologists had been summoned to spur the Queen to further effort, but Dame Alice had no such problems and Sir Thomas pronounced himself satisfied by her wifely charms in an explicit Latin inscription on their funeral monument, which was ordered in advance and can still be seen in Chelsea Old Church.

The next botanical innovator was Sir Hans Sloane, who became Lord of the Manor in 1712. As President of the Royal College of Physicians, he had grown progressively more irritated by the incompetence of apothecaries, who mixed up prescrip-tions, often with lethal results. As a young man, Sir Hans went to the West Indies and brought back *thebroma cacao*, the cocoa plant. He prescribed it as a laxative, but also invented a deli-cious drink, 'Sir Hans Sloane's Milk Chocolate' recommended for its 'lightness on the stomach and its great use in all consumptive cases'. Chocolate drinking became popular as a result.

In the interests of improving the nation's health, Sir Hans bought up the Physic Garden, which the Apothecaries Company had mismanaged since 1673. He granted them the freehold on condition they should present annually fifty new plants to the Royal Society. The Physic Garden became a hive of horticultural endeavour and the apothecaries erected a marble statue of Sir Hans in the centre. They also established a library with a proper system for cataloguing botanical specimens. Two ancient cedar trees still dominate the Physic Garden and its herb-filled walks are open to the public on Wednesday and Sunday afternoons.

The trees are Lebanon cedars and it was while sitting in their shade that Daphne Macdonald, a great gardener of our time, felt the urge to redesign the garden of St Andrew's Church, Park Walk. Mrs Macdonald was a distinguished and tireless worker. She toiled selflessly for Gardening for the Disabled and was the self-appointed Head Gardener at St Andrew's, when it was so overgrown that no one else would take on the job. To help with her new scheme she called in the highly professional Sylvia Taylor, who immediately suggested that they should make a Bible Garden. Daphne knew one of the curators at Kew who had just written a book about Bible Gardens so the project quickly got under way.

Sylvia lived in Chelsea at the time and was considered avant-garde, having just created vistas of box trees at Anoushka Hempel's then latest venture, Blake's Hotel. Her earlier career had involved finding film locations and she had been caught up in a fierce dispute over crossing Westminster Bridge with six camels that were needed for a shoot. Lambeth Council, who controlled the southern section had been totally co-operative, but Westminster, who felt they had a prestigious reputation to maintain, refused point blank to have camels wandering about in the vicinity of Scotland Yard. 'To put it in a nutshell,' said Sylvia, 'they were absolutely bloody.'

The Bible Garden seemed welcome therapy. Sylvia liked Daphne's direct approach. She had rung one evening with the simple introduction, 'I hear you're a member of the Hardy Plants Society. I think I'm going to need your help.'

It was felt that because the venture was for charity, costs should be cut, wherever possible. Mr Macdonald was roped in as Head of Forestry. He was discovered one morning practising tree surgery in Park Walk by a suspicious-minded policeman, who tried to arrest him for wilful damage. When the mild-mannered Ranald Macdonald explained he had the Vicar's permission to cut down the tree, he was asked to name the Vicar. At the reply 'John Smith', he was marched straight off to the Chelsea Police Station. When it transpired that the Vicar was indeed called John Smith, the former Governor of a large chunk of the British Raj was released with apologies.

The next misadventure was a direct result of Daphne's cost cutting. The two ladies had decided to build a pond and had found a disused bath on a skip in Elm Park Gardens. With unparalleled goodwill they lugged it down Fulham Road and began to dig a hole. Unfortunately, just as the hole was nearing completion, a story broke in all the tabloids that some unauthorized grave-diggers had been burying human remains in a Church of England parish in south west London. The crowds who collected in Park Walk were phenomenal.

7
All in Bloom

Independently of the orchards and flower walks laid out by the nobility, Chelsea was an area of market gardens. Farmers, small-holders and pretty wenches carried baskets of fruit and vegetables daily to London. Present-day Tryon Street was a passage between two large gardens. Honeysuckle grew along one side and the air was so heavily scented that it drew swarms of small insects. The narrow lane became known as Butterfly Alley. By the eighteenth century Chelsea was renowned for finely painted bone china, decorated not only with flowers and tendrils, but also with butterflies, bees and dragonflies.

In Charles II's time, Chelsea strawberries were famous for their size and flavour. Pepys loved to steal away from his office at the Admiralty to eat a dish of them in a tavern by the river. If he could get Mrs Knipp, his favourite actress, to accompany him, so much the better. The biographer John Aubrey thought strawberries 'so innocent a woman in childbed, or one with a fever, may safely eat them', but he had heard from Sir Christopher Wren, a notorious food faddist, that if anyone had a head wound,' 'strawberries would be mortal'.

Chelsea was fast becoming a popular pleasure resort. By the middle of his reign King Charles II, who tended to think of it as his own private bathing place, surveyed the swinging scene and remarked acidly that it was getting like 'Hyde Park by the Thames'. Many gentlefolk had gone to live there, building houses with large private gardens, where exotic fruits such as figs and medlars were cultivated alongside the peaches and 'apricocks' beloved by the Elizabethans. But it was the flowers tumbling in scented profusion over brick walls, or growing at random in the meadows, which gave the riverside village its feeling of perpetual spring.

In the eighteenth century, tulip mania broke out in Chelsea as frantically as anywhere else. Collectors would pay as much as 1,000 guineas for a single bulb and often tulips would be used as currency instead of coin of the realm. Long after the craze had subsided rare species were cultivated in the King's Road nurseries. In Queen Victoria's reign there was a grower whose catalogue included a single recherché bulb at 200 guineas. With continuous classification going on in the Physic Garden, botany and horticulture flourished side by side. Shortly after Sir Hans Sloane had laid his edict upon the Apothecaries to present fifty new species each year to the Royal Society, the great Swedish botanist Carl Linnaeus arrived in England. He had studied the sex life of plants and invented a new method of classification which was so successful it is still used today. Linnaeus announced that he would catalogue all nature from buffaloes to buttercups. As Lord of the Manor and President of the Royal Society, Sir Hans welcomed him warmly, but he soon found the famous Swede a crashing bore.

Despite the discovery that plants had a sex life, botany became a respectable study for ladies. Elizabeth Blackwell, a gifted water-colourist who lived at 4 Swan Walk, heard that pictures were urgently needed to help identify all the new plants which were being discovered. Her drawings delighted Sir Hans and Dr Rand, the Curator of the Physic Garden. She was engaged to produce *A Curious Herbal*, which listed the five hundred most useful plants used in contemporary medicine. Some time later, Queen Charlotte took to drawing flowers as therapy against the madness of George III. Endorsed by royalty, the subject became increasingly popular and every new species was welcomed excitedly by both nurserymen and scientists. In 1822 there was tremendous approbation when a Mr Davies produced the first-ever red geranium at Chelsea.

By the close of the eighteenth century half of all the vegetables sold in Covent Garden were grown in Chelsea. Two nurseries dominated the King's Road: Colvill's, which extended from Blackland's Lane to the present King's Walk Shopping Mall and Davey's, which stretched towards Markham Square. Colvill's had a conservatory with ingenious under-floor heating. At one time it housed five hundred species of geranium and a fascinated public flocked to behold the spectacle. Further down the King's Road, near Flood Street, Humphrey Richard Taylor grew roses and lavender and set up a perfume distillery which survived until 1852. There was also a nursery beside the Queen's Elm which later moved to World's End.

In or near each place where a nursery once stood, there is now, by a strange coincidence, a flower stall splashing colour and vitality onto the grey London pavements. The King's Road boasts three. The largest is beside the Duke of York's Territorial Army Headquarters opposite Peter Jones and it has a little glass office, where the florist can shelter on a rainy day. The grandest is Osborne's by Wellington Square, a family business which has been manned by father and son for twenty years. The Osbornes purvey out-of-season mimosa to incognito duchesses. Their elegant display under green and white awnings is much photographed by foreign tourists as a 'scene from Chelsea life'.

Further down, on the corner of Chelsea Manor Street, 'John the Flowers' has been setting up his stall beside the Post Office for longer than most people can remember. He is a daffodils and anemones man, scorning mixed bunches. If his customers want him to make up a bouquet, that's a different matter: he will do so but *they* must choose the flowers. He does not pretend to be an arbiter of taste. John pitches his stall at nine o'clock every morning and then drinks a pint of lager to set himself up for the day. His name is John Colwick but no one ever calls him anything but 'John the Flowers'. He remembers Covent Garden Market when it was WC2, not Nine Elms, and his customers include dozens of celebrities. He sold tulips to Joanna Lumley in the era before *Ab. Fab* made it imperative for her to shop in dark glasses.

At the next corner, opposite Heal's and near the junction of

King's Road and Sydney Street, is the Chelsea Gardener. It was started by Major Fenwick in 1984 and stands beside the Farmer's Market. Green-fingered ladies bustle in and out wearing Barbours. Their daughters often go there for genteel work experience after completing GCSEs. You can buy anything at the Gardener from a twelve-foot palm to an autumn crocus. The premises are spacious and, under the capable management of Daphne Dormer, they are used for evening parties, once recently by the Prince of Wales's Architectural Trust. The shop used to be full of English matrons in search of a little bit of *rus in urbe*, but as it now stocks almost every flower-seed that was ever classified, the clientèle has become more global. People from abroad carry off thousands of pounds' worth of seeds to create cottage gardens in all sorts of unsuitable climates and even the Duchess of Devonshire shops there.

At weekends, when the English flock to the country, the Gardener is filled with French people and Italians in search of *le style anglais.* A recent feat was the selling of a palm tree to a Saudi Arabian gentleman who wanted to take it back to Riyadh. On Mondays the Brits all troop back again, rejuvenated from the country air. The spirit of Empire prevails as highly polished Range Rovers pull up outside in flagrant disregard of the parking regulations. I once stood mesmerized, watching a blue-rinsed lady load six gardenias into the passenger seat of a Bentley, while, simultaneously, a clamping unit immobilized her front wheel on the driver's side.

Another colourful florist is Mr Bolton in the Fulham Road, who has an impressive pitch outside the Queen's Elm. He stocks a great deal of curly willow as well as a lovely selection of blooms and he is a High Apostle of foliage. In the autumn his hypericum berries are a *sine qua non* of the decorating world. They have been photographed in *Interiors* and appear poking out of burnished copper vessels at all the best Antique Fairs, but the most loved and longest established of the Fulham Road flower-sellers are Lynne and Mick Rayment, who have run the Callow Street barrow for twenty-eight years.

Callow Street is in that fashionable part of 'Little Chelsea' known as the Beach, where personalities of both sexes go to see and be seen. It is a parade in the old-fashioned sense of the word and the dress code is flamboyant. It lacks the calculated chic of the King's Road, but in the laid-back and highly creative milieu of SW10 startling ensembles seem to put themselves together. No one bats an eyelid, but patrons of the Callow Street barrow tend to be as colourful as the flowers themselves.

A few shops on the Beach sell the necessities of life like stamps and bread and washers for leaking taps. They are vastly outnumbered, however, by the places where people go simply to drink coffee, wine, lager or well-chilled coke. The Pan Book Shop, the Café Délice, the Goat in Boots and the UGC Cinema are just a few of the local amenities. Aubergine, London's currently most crowded restaurant, is just round the corner. Its owner, Gordon Ramsay, the shouting chef, was voted the rudest man in television. Further down Fulham Road is Joel Cadbury's VQ – vingt-quatre – a twenty-four-hour scene, where breakfast is served at 4 a.m. when clubbers and gamblers troop in.

Actors, artists, patrons of Aubergine and ex-patriate Americans on their way back from working out at the Holmes Place Fitness Centre all frequent the Beach, so Lynne and Mick are assured of a star-spangled clientèle. Hugh Grant, Kylie Minogue, Nigel Havers, Susan Hampshire and Michael Jackson have all shopped at the Callow Street barrow, though they are not necessarily the biggest spenders. When the cinema, which has had seven changes of ownership in eighteen years, was owned by Virgin, Richard Branson would turn up to matinées unannounced. He rarely got beyond the usherettes without being recognized, at which point Patrick, the assistant manager, would rush across to the barrow to buy hundreds of pounds' worth of red roses to decorate the Gents' loo. Even his order was surpassed the night the landlord of the Goat in Boots got engaged. Red and white roses were ordered by the bucketful and the massive outlay is still spoken of in awed tones.

Because of its location, the stall attracts a great many titled ladies. They shop in head-scarves and know a ranunculus when they see one. The-people-who-ski with the Prince of Wales are also customers. Americans who recognize them choosing their longhi lilies think it is tantamount to a Royal Appointment. Lynne never tires of making spectacular bouquets in glowing colours and the barrow, which is trundled away to its overnight quarters at 8 p.m. is renowned for its social life. Many regulars do not come so much to buy flowers as for the conversation, which is of a high order. There are some very superior florists in Callow Street: resting actresses mind the stall on Tuesdays and Fridays, while Graham the Transport Manager and Chief Public Relations Executive makes sporadic appearances through the day. His Rory Bremner imitations are without equal and he also does a very good Austin Powers.

Chelsea Chicks linger by the barrow, drawn by its mesmeric social status. They come swinging their Prada bags and hang about with mobile phones. They come wearing paint-stained overalls to buy one gerbera daisy, which they want to sketch against a sunset. They come for bunches of anemones for their office desks. Some arrive with a rich boyfriend in tow who buys them armfuls of lizzianthus. Wearing the latest in thigh-split skirts and the tightest of jeans, they eye Graham provocatively through lightly mascaraed lashes until the boyfriends pay up and hurry them along. In the spring, when the Transport Executive wears his designer shorts, there is an immediate leap in the takings. He is thinking of insuring his legs.

The annual climax of the floral calendar is the Royal Horticultural Society's Show. Held in the grounds of the Royal Hospital since 1913, it is the most famous flower show in the world. Hampton Court has a bigger one, with better parking, but the RHS still regards Chelsea as its flagship. The atmosphere is quintessentially British. Chelsea Chicks decked out in 'style anglais' hats compete with the blooms. The Pensioners put on their red coats and a Guards band plays a selection from *Lilac Time*. The Queen comes in a motorcade. Visiting Americans arrive in tour buses, having timed their vacations to coincide with the event. Attendance last year was 170,000 and the crowds brought traffic to a standstill.

They come with their Prada bags and hang about with mobile phones.

Coincidentally Sir Simon Hornby, who as President of the RHS, pilots the Queen round before the first day, is also the Chairman of the Chelsea Society, so for the most part traditional rituals are observed. From time to time, however, the Great Marquee wears out. You cannot expect a field tent to last eighty-seven years. The last one spanned three and a half acres and got into the *Guinness Book of Records*, but for the Millennium a new one has been designed in white pvc and extruded aluminium. The lay-out includes two new avenues which allow spectacular views of the Royal Hospital. Sir Christopher Wren would have approved.

The birth of the RHS was the result of a wonderfully Etonian piece of savoir faire. As a boy Sir Joseph Bank, the founder, lived on the corner of Paradise Row, nearly opposite the Physic Garden. In the school holidays he went there to sit at the feet of Philip Miller, who was known as 'the Prince of Gardeners'. Later, as an adventurous and wealthy young man, Banks sailed with Captain Cook to search for Australia. En route he amassed botanical specimens which, when Australia was finally located, were spread out to dry on a sail laid on a beach in New South Wales. Banks, a fastidious traveller who part-financed the expedition, had set out with two artists, two white servants, two black servants and two dogs. The beach with the specimens was named Botany Bay, but Banks considered the facilities there a little primitive. On his return he founded the RHS to give botanists a better deal.

Nowadays it takes three weeks to prepare the Hospital grounds for the Flower Show. A four-mile water system has to be installed, with tanks holding up to 20,000 gallons. The catering is done in Ranelagh Gardens. In the refreshment tents, champagne consumption is reputed to be higher than in Ascot Week and someone has calculated that 8,000 sandwiches were washed down last year by 60,000 cups of tea. As we have observed, the Flower Show is quintessentially English. The rose growers always hog the front page of *The Times*. The Queen Mother and Susan Hampshire do sterling work, smelling exhibits for the photographers. It is better to snap an old pro than a nouveau celebrity, because they get the tilt of the head right and don't let their hats obscure the blooms. 'You couldn't', says a *Telegraph* man, 'risk Madonna sniffing a lily. She wouldn't get the angle right. It takes years of practice. Even Diana wasn't a patch on that lovely Queen Mum.'

Although many people 'go for the atmosphere' a lot stay away to enjoy a thoroughly good grumble. Ticket-holders, they say, cannot see the flowers any more because of the crowds, but the Gala Evening is still wildly oversubscribed and a last-minute ballot is held to apportion the tickets. They are £200 each and the proceeds go to fashionable charities.

Local residents react variously. Nigel says because of the crowds the only solution is 'to ditch the car and walk'. Most people do. Basia Briggs, who lives in Sloane Gardens – 'normally the quietest street in England' – says she stands at her window in Flower Show week watching thousands of people troop past her front door, as each tube train disgorges a new cargo of flower-lovers into Sloane Square. 'They come from all over Britain,' she says. 'You can't take the dog out. It gets too traumatized.' At the end of the day they all troop back again. Traffic is gridlocked and access blocked to Basia's front door, even though the Met drafts in hundreds of extra policemen. On the last day when the exhibits are sold, people grin from ear to ear as they trudge along 'clutching a five-foot delphinium'. Lady Longford once went as a guest of royalty. 'The first and only time I ever travelled in a motorcade,' she said. 'It was a quite extraordinary sensation to see the King's Road empty magically before us, as the outriders went ahead. Then through the chauffeur's mirror you could see the crowds closing in behind.'

8
Fauna

Chelsea folk have a mania for keeping unusual pets. Lady More's monkey was part of a menagerie which Sir Thomas began to assemble when, as a young man, he lived at Bucklersbury in the heart of the City. There the animals were kept in cages, but when the Mores moved to their spacious new estate by the river, they were allowed to roam freely. In the 1860s the artist Dante Gabriel Rossetti staunchly upheld the tradition of giving animals plenty of space, keeping armadillos, kangaroos, squirrels, mice, dormice, two owls and a racoon in the garden of his house in Cheyne Walk. The armadillos promptly burrowed into other people's gardens and one came up through the kitchen floor of a neighbouring house, sending the cook into hysterics; the peacocks flew into the trees, screaming hideously in the mating season and the neighbours complained so frequently that the Cadogan Estates inserted a clause in the leases, expressly forbidding the keeping of peacocks in Cheyne Walk, which applies to this day.

Rossetti's most famous pet was a wombat, which was sketched by William Bell Scott and 'Rossetti's Wombat Seated on his Lap' can now be seen in the Tate Gallery. Ellen Terry once arrived at Cheyne Walk to find the painter had just bought a white bull. 'He tethered it on the lawn,' she wrote. 'Soon there was no lawn left – only the bull. He invited people to meet it, and heaped favours on it until it kicked everything to pieces.'

Perhaps it is an addiction to the Higher Bohemianism which makes Chelsea people accident-prone when it comes to pets.

Doctor Emina Kurtagic, that Sibyl of Oakley Street who, it will be remembered, was told that she had the soul of a fish, bought a cockateel and named him Attar after a fourteenth-century Persian poet. When Attar died, he was replaced by a second bird, known as Attar the Great, who was destined for stardom. One morning Emina was breakfasting with a musician whom she had asked to compose a theme for her forthcoming video about a Russian flower painter. Attar the Great had been allowed to fly free and Emina was somewhat alarmed when the bird alighted on the young man's shoulder, and began pecking his earring. She had trained Attar not to do this, being herself the owner of a fine collection of old Croatian jewellery, some of which had belonged to her grandmother. On this occasion, however, Attar's instincts overcame his training and, quick as a flash, he detached a large chunk of the earring and swallowed it whole. The breakfast party broke up immediately and Attar was rushed to the Blue Cross Animals Hospital in Victoria. A documentary film-team had just arrived from ITV and they recorded part of the operation by which the earring was removed. Attar recovered instantly and flew about the room, zooming and diving uninhibitedly before the cameras. He became extremely famous, while Dr Kurtagic, who had been longing to break into British television ever since she left Zagreb, basked in his reflected glory. The young musician got no publicity at all, gave up wearing earrings and has since become a commissioning editor for an Associated Newspaper handbook about Euromoney.

Owing to the large number of dog-owners in Chelsea, strict rules prevail about animal behaviour at the Royal Hospital. Biters and brawlers are excluded, but well-behaved dogs can be promenaded in Ranelagh Gardens, provided they conform to the hygiene rules. All dogs, however, are banned during Flower Show Week. Occasionally, world-famous super models have got away with smuggling in a chihuahua in a handbag, but this is frowned upon. Unaccountably, nobody thought of legislating against rabbits and, on the first day of last year's Chelsea Flower Show, one was scheduled to shoot through an exhibit described as 'Mr McGregor's Garden' for a press call.

The rabbit escaped early and the photographers arrived late. Pandemonium ensued. The escapee, far from being frightened by the crowds, put in various appearances through the day. By noon he was a celebrity, his progress monitored by the BBC. Immediately he was sighted, or even when it was *thought* he was sighted, he was trailed by a posse of photographers from the tabloids. Mr McGregor's Garden was in the south section near the Bull Ring Gate, however, so two worries soon prevailed. One was that the rabbit might bolt for the Embankment and be run over or drowned in the Thames. The other was that he would escape into the Great Marquee, where the *Evening Standard* and Laurent Perrier, the champagne people, had a prestigious exhibit designed by Sir Terence Conran. Entitled 'The Chef's Roof Garden' it featured 'vegetables, fruit, flowers and herbs full of flavour', all supplied by a Mr Chewter.

It is a well-known fact that news photographers will stoop to anything in Flower Show Week. The posse from the *Standard* took up strategic positions inside the Great Marquee, hoping the rabbit would turn out to be a herbivorous gourmet, who would treat Mr Chewter's garden like a miniature version of Sir Terence's Gastrodome. Rival photographers, meanwhile, stationed themselves outside the marquee. It is believed that some of the tabloid regulars were even prepared to catch the rabbit in order to divert it from the *Standard*'s showpiece. There are at least six different accounts of how the story ended, including one about an inebriated bunny happily nibbling crudités marinated in champagne. An informed source puts the blame on Laurent Perrier's press office.

Another rabbit notorious in the annals of SW3 keeps gnawing through Lady Wynne Jones's telephone wire, thus becoming a permanent headache for the BT Engineers. Lady Wynne-Jones, better known to her friends as Rasheen, is the owner of Chelsea's last surviving outdoor aviary. She is a committed campaigner and was heavily involved in saving the Albert Bridge and Tedworth Square. She would have saved the House of Lords too, if only they had left it to *her*, but as a Peer's widow she was not entitled to voting rights. It is also difficult to maintain a high political profile when you are hampered by a White Rabbit with an obsessive hatred of incoming calls.

Rasheen's aviary runs vertically down the façade of her terraced cottage near Chelsea Green. It is one of the sights of the district and is supported by a live willow tree and a silver poplar, surrounded by a cascade of tumbling foliage. The inhabitants of the spacious cage, which runs the whole breadth of the upper storey, are song-birds of species which prefer to breed in captivity and they chirrup cheerfully as they fly in and out of the small bird-houses. Beneath the aviary a vertically organized woodland garden includes a *trompe l'oeil* selection of natural and artificial plants. At Christmas-time the house is televised for the charity Warchild. To the delight of disabled children garden sculptures which would not disgrace the Disneyland Rides are tastefully arranged at intervals. A contemplative frog sits on a toadstool, a swan perches by a small waterfall and a stone owl peers wisely out over Elystan Street. Outside the front door a broomstick leans beneath a notice proclaiming 'Honey for Sale' and fairy lights are hung over all.

Taxi drivers describe Elystan Street as 'the scenic route'. They take Japanese tourists there to hear the waterfall plashing, but Rasheen deeply resents the suggestion that she is Chelsea's eccentric bird-woman. When she bought the house in 1994, she had, as a qualified lawyer, just defended the owner of an aviary. The next day he brought her eight fairy bluebirds, knowing her to be a keen protector of endangered species. On moving into the house she discovered her lease included grazing rights to Chelsea Green which dated back to Magna Carta and she sounded out the neighbours to see whether they would mind her tethering a goat there. She belongs to several societies for the preservation of rare species and was for some time the owner of two Arctic squirrels. One had 'a nature like Houdini' and performed astonishing feats of escapology.

On a particularly memorable occasion the buyer of Peter Jones's haberdashery department telephoned.

'Milady, are you missing anything?'

'I don't think so. Why?'

'We have a sort of white rat here and the customers think it's vermin.'

She replied with some asperity that an Arctic squirrel was first cousin to a mink. She supposed the customers meant 'ermine', but she went to PJ to retrieve the offending animal. Unfortunately, it had run amok in 'Ribbons and Trimmings' and had managed to wind itself into a few yards of exquisite lace, so that it looked like a forlorn and furry bride. On another occasion the same creature ran along the window sills of an adjacent house and got into bed beside its sleeping owner. An astonished window-cleaner looked through the casement to see the affectionate little animal nestling beside a man in striped pyjamas. A few minutes later the wanton beast decided to go home and popped out through another window. It was too much for the window-cleaner. He lost his balance and dropped his pail.

It goes without saying that standards of pet care are high. There are two veterinary surgeons in Chelsea and both believe firmly in preventive medicine. Mr Clifford of the Brompton Clinic practises in the Fulham Road. He gives the Park Walk cats their flu jabs and has recently taken on a partner who specializes in homoeopathic remedies for dogs. Mr O'Neill runs the Chelsea Clinic in Blacklands Terrace. He has been there for fifty years and is interested in treating older pets. He prescribes life-prolonging vitamins and gentle retraining programmes for animals coping with the traumas of ageing. In an area where women get younger every day, swearing by organic foodstuffs, green-lipped mussels and relentless work-outs at Holmes Place Health Club, pet-owners expect their animals to be food conscious.

In the 1970s there was a celebrated case of an anorexic python, which lived in Elm Park Gardens. Its owners, assured by the pet shop that it would eat only once a week, grew anxious when a live grey mouse which had been placed in the snake's cage was happily co-habiting with it six weeks later. They telephoned the Zoo and were informed that if the python continued to refuse to eat the mouse, sooner or later the mouse would eat the python, beginning with its tail. Another authority suggested they should change the colour of the mouse, since pythons are sometimes fussy eaters. A white mouse was immediately placed in the cage. It was as though the python had been offered a choice between McDonald's in the King's Road and a free meal at Aubergine. It devoured the white mouse without further ado.

Stories of rats and mice pale into insignificance, however, beside the true tale of Fiona, the butterflies and the Royal Bank of Scotland. She had been invited to fund-raise for the Royal Entomological Society – during the year that they organized an expedition to Indonesia to observe rare butterflies. She approached Williams & Glynn's Bank in the Old Brompton Road, where an affable man who seemed to be the manager promised to sponsor a promotion: the entire front window of the Bank would feature a display of live butterflies. The staff of the Royal Entomological Society were delighted by such glamorous publicity. It was agreed that the display would be kept at a suitable temperature and sealed off from the rest of the bank by a glass partition. As the day of the promotion approached the front of the bank began to fill up with tropical plants and exotic flora. A whole lorry-load of peat was delivered to facilitate planting.

The day before the butterflies were due to arrive the Royal Entomological Society received a phone call. 'What do you mean', a voice asked peevishly, 'by filling my bank with bags of peat?'

'You said we could.'

'I said no such thing.'

To the acute embarrassment of the entomologists it transpired that the *real* bank manager had been on holiday. The man who had given the go-ahead was an assistant manager who had been fired but was working out his notice. Fiona was sent to plead in person. She was a striking beauty, a Chelsea Chick of the first order. At the sight of her anxious face framed by the red-gold pre-Raphaelite hair, the real bank manager's heart melted. He would be delighted, he said, to sponsor a display for such a distinguished body.

The window was filled with peat. The plants were installed. The butterflies fluttered happily in their new environment. The bank manager beamed satisfaction – until he learned that the Banana Butterfly was so called because it had to be fed bananas every day, even on Sundays. As the unfortunate man toiled up from his home in South London to open the premises, even the sight of Fiona's Pre-Raphaelite mane began to pall. Nor was that the end of the story. The premises which had been Williams & Glynn's Bank were due to be taken over by the Royal Bank of Scotland. In the general ferment someone left the glass partition which screened the window from the bank ajar and the new directors held their first meeting surrounded by fluttering fauna. Fiona left the Royal Entomological Society before discovering whether the Indonesian expedition was a success.

In a village like Chelsea, where many people feel strongly about Animal Rights, fur-wearing has now waned. This is not so in countries north of the Arctic meridian. Mink-coated Swedes and Russian beauties swathed in sable are hurt and puzzled by the dirty looks they receive, while shopping in Marks & Spencer in the King's Road. In less humane times a great many ladies wore fur coats to Walton's, the restaurant near Brompton Cross, patronised by Mrs Thatcher and occasionally by the Queen Mother, until it was blown up by the IRA. A transvestite film producer, doubling as a waiter, used to slip into the ladies' cloakroom and try on the minks and sables during his breaks. He would mix up the pelts which the coat check girl had hung on numbered pegs. Customers who had walked in wearing mink wraps, would occasionally be amazed to be offered a full length Arctic fox, as they were about to leave.

A fur-wearing episode *de nos jours* occurred when Kay Campbell-Johnson flew in from Rome, where mink is still lovingly tolerated. On a cold dark night she decided to wrap up warmly for a lecture at the Royal Geographical Society. She knew the risks but was prepared to brave them. Just as she was on her way home she heard footsteps behind her and women's

directly over the river. Its inhabitants have always been the rich or the privileged and their women have lived colourful lives.

Lady Jane Cheyne was almost a saint and certainly a story-book heroine. During the Civil War, she was besieged by the Roundheads in her father's house at Welbeck. He escaped, but she and her sisters remained in England throughout the Interregnum. At the Restoration she sold all her jewels to bring her father back from exile in Rotterdam. She was famously char-itable and endowed Chelsea Old Church. At her death in 1669 the entire parish mourned. Lord Cheyne had worshipped her. He commissioned a monument from Paolo Bernini, the son of the celebrated architect who had designed part of the Vatican. Antonio Raggi, one of the best sculptors in Rome, was employed to carve a likeness from Carrara marble to be placed in the Old Church, where it stands today.

Because she was a Duke's daughter, it was suggested that Lady Jane should be represented for posterity with a coronet on her head. The Italian sculptor was profoundly shocked by this idea. Only Mary Queen of Heaven could be represented with a crown, he informed Lord Cheyne's agent; not even the saints were entitled to such a thing. Back went the reply to Rome: Lady Jane was an ardent Protestant. The rules did not apply. She was the daughter of an English Duke and a coronet was required by armorial custom. In the end the sculptor, who had become quite temperamental, placed a coronet at her feet, to indicate that Lady Jane, although entitled to wear such a thing in life, would have scorned it deeply by the time she qualified for heav-enly raiment.

Lord Cheyne's second wife was the widowed Countess of Radnor, Laetitia Isabella, who had been one of the dazzling beauties of Charles II's court. She was much fancied by the King's brother, the Duke of York, but Lord Radnor, an elderly peer described by one contemporary as 'an old snarling, trou-blesome, peevish fellow', had been a possessive husband. The Radnors had taken Danvers House, a bijou property west of the Old Manor with an Italian garden which swept down to the river. It had been created by Sir John Danvers and was much admired by Aubrey, who claimed it was the first of its kind in England. The dining-room faced south, opening on to a balustrade which looked down on 'a boscage of lilacs, syringas and sweet briar'. Beyond it was a herb garden, where Sir John would brush his beaver hat against the rosemary bushes until it had collected enough scent to last a morning.

He had married Magdalen Herbert, a widow twice his age, and Danvers House echoed to the laughter of seven stepchildren, the fifth of whom was the poet George Herbert. Lady Danvers must have been a tolerant soul. Izaak Walton was a regular house guest. The Compleat Angler would arrive with a complete range of fishing tackle to clutter the tiny house, for the Thames was as yet unpolluted and plentifully stocked with salmon, trout, bream and every other freshwater delicacy. Sir John was probably the originator of the garden gnome for, instead of decorating his 'boscage' with half-clothed classical statuary pillaged from the Grand Tour, he erected stone models of his gardener and housekeeper in rustic dress. Despite its amenities, the house held no happy memories for Laetitia Radnor. As soon as her bad-tempered Earl died, she moved to one of the spacious new houses in Paradise Row, opposite the Royal Hospital. The Row, which was to deteriorate into a dreadful slum in the next century, had undoubted prestige in Stuart times though, of course, it lacked the cachet of Cheyne Walk. When Charles Cheyne proposed, therefore, Laetitia cheerfully dropped her status as Dowager Countess in exchange for a common Viscount, a happy marriage and a more meritorious address.

Lord Cheyne owned most of the houses in Paradise Row and, shortly after Charles II's death, he leased one to the King's last mistress, Hortense Mancini, Duchess of Mazarin, whom the new government wished to evict from her 'petit palais' in St James's. As a girl, Hortense had been in love with Charles Stuart, then a penniless exile in Paris. However, her uncle, the all-powerful French Finance Minister, Cardinal Mazarin, refused to let her marry the heir to the English throne and he arranged a match for her with the mad Duc de Meilleraye, who changed his name to Mazarin. After the marriage the Duke's madness increased. He suffered from the delusion that he was a tulip. He locked Hortense in a convent, where she was supervised by devout nuns, but she managed to escape disguised as a boy and arrived in England, where her cousin was Duchess of York.

With the avowed intention of becoming Charles II's mistress, Hortense continued provocatively to dress in men's clothes until she came to the notice of the King. She was extremely beautiful and Charles, delighted both by her loveliness and her spirit of adventure, gave her a house in St James's and an allowance of £4,000 a year. Louise de Kerouaille was furious but Nell Gwyn, noticing a slight irregularity about the young woman's eyes, accepted her with amusement and nicknamed her Squintarella.

After Charles's death Hortense remained in England, an enchanting salonnière with no visible means of support. She was unemployed and unemployable. As a Duchess turned royal mistress she had no experience of the ancillary professions. There were questions in parliament. It was even suggested that she should be shipped back to France, but she was admired by the elderly Chevalier de Saint-Evremond whom Charles, in a moment of playfulness, had created Governor of Duck Island. Although this was in the middle of St James's Park, a small salary went with the post. Hortense's soirées were so delightful and her table so excellent that she quickly slipped into the role of a professional party-planner. Her friends would come to dinner and tactfully slide money under the plates. She kept many animals, had a passion for parrots and monkeys and was the first in Chelsea's long line of Bohemians. When she died her husband had her body sent back to France. 'At last,' wrote John Evelyn 'the Duchess of Mazarin is to be interred with her ancestors.' In fact the deranged Duke had her embalmed and carried her about with him wherever he went.

Old Lord Cheyne died in 1698 and William, his son by Lady Jane, inherited the Manor. Laetitia promptly moved back to Paradise Row, which was by then more fashionable than when she had first lived there on account of the beau monde who had flocked to Hortense's parties. The new Viscount Cheyne was a country squire with little interest in London matters, being chiefly concerned with his Buckinghamshire estates. Feeling he had duties to his Chelsea tenantry, however, he built Cheyne Row in 1708, a terrace of modestly priced houses for folk whose incomes would not stretch to the luxury of a home by the river. Poor William. He immediately incurred the wrath of urban conservationists for destroying a bowling green and creating an eyesore. Disillusioned by philanthropy he sold the Manor to Sir Hans Sloane and returned to the rustic delights of Chesham Bois.

The new landlord had no qualms about selling off land. Of the eighteen acres he bought from Lord Cheyne, Sloane retained only two, planting them, in the opinion of Edmund Howard, his gardener and odd-job man, with 'some very bad tulips' and roots which 'a country dame would scarce have allowed place'. Strip by strip Henry VIII's Great Garden fell to the developers. Sir Hans and Lady Sloane used the Old Manor House only at weekends, because he remained in practice as a doctor until 1742, living in Bloomsbury during the week. Sloane was physician to Queen Anne, George I and George II. Queen Caroline thought the world of him and when it was certain that the treatment was safe, she had him inoculate the royal children against smallpox. Despite treating the most fashionable invalids in London, Sloane also saw poor patients, providing they arrived at his consulting rooms before 10 a.m. President both of the Royal Society and the Royal College of Physicians, he did not retire from medicine until he was eighty-two.

In common with most of his contemporaries, Sloane sometimes adopted drastic remedies as when he ordered Queen Anne to be bled on her deathbed, but he also believed in holistic medicine. Counting fresh air among the most important things in life, he would bundle the Bloomsbury household into his carriage every weekend and they would all go bowling along the country lanes to Chelsea. Lady Sloane must have been a remarkable woman. She was the widow of Fulk Rose, a Jamaican planter, and brought four stepdaughters to her second marriage. She bore four more children for Sir Hans, of whom two survived. The youngest, Elizabeth, married Charles Cadogan, who succeeded his father-in-law as Lord of the Manor. Sloane's grandson, another Charles Cadogan, was the first Viscount Chelsea and brought the waterside village into the Cadogan family.

The first land sold by Sir Hans was the river frontage on the eastern side of Cheyne Walk. John Witt began to build there in 1717, putting up rose-red brick houses with dependable sanitation and a water supply from the conduit at Kensington. Certain status symbols indicated that residents of the Walk would be a cut above their neighbours in Cheyne Row. The earlier development boasted small alcoves in which a pageboy could sleep whereas the houses in the Walk had large powder closets where the family valet could dress wigs, seated if he so chose at a table. The professional classes and minor gentry were swift to move in.

The largest house in the Walk was No. 6. It had four reception rooms, two dining-rooms and thirteen bedrooms – an obvious requirement for a family with such superior servants. Here Dr Dominicetti, an Italian entrepreneur, spent the astronomical sum of £37,000 installing a steam bath with thirty-six sweating and fumigatory chambers. Smart patients flocked to take his cure. Some thought him a quack, but he had a high rate of success with asthma and rheumatic cases. His grandest patient was the Duke of York. Chelsea's obsession with high-class health-care had begun.

Cheyne Walk retained a façade of respectability through the eighteenth century, though by the nineteenth it had a right and a wrong end. Its amenities included Don Saltero's famous Coffee House, patronized by Addison, Swift and Steele. 'Don Saltero' was James Slater, an irrepressible Irishman, who had been Sir Hans Sloane's valet. Steele wrote him a comic puff in the *Tatler*, which was read with mirth throughout London. Sir Hans had gone to the West Indies in 1687 with the Duke of Albemarle, the new Governor of Jamaica. He returned with 800 botanical specimens, which soon formed part of the great collection he left to the nation and which was to be the foundation of the British Museum.

Slater started a collection of his own, a parody of his master's. The exhibits ranged from pickled snakes to 'Queen Elizabeth's Prayer Book, strawberry cup and riding stirrup'. There were trophies from afar such as the 'rattle of a rattlesnake' and relics of popery including a 'nun's whip' and a model of the Holy Sepulchre inlaid with mother of pearl. Customers donated curiosities and from time to time a list of donors was printed. It ran from old sea-faring men to the Duke of Buccleuch. The Coffee House also operated as a barber's shop and dental clinic.

It was flanked by two notable taverns, the Six Bells, later frequented by Whistler, which is still flourishing and the Magpie and Stump, a hostelry established by the waterside even before Henry VIII bought the Manor House. In medieval times it doubled as a court-leet, the forerunner of that fearsome department of the RBKC which determines Council Tax. Fees and dues were collected twice yearly. Henry allowed it to retain its own strip of land within the confines of his estate and grazing for one heifer on Chelsea Common. It remained in use as a tavern until the 1880s, when the present 37 Cheyne Walk was built and it was painted by Whistler's pupil Walter Greaves.

The Victorians prized the Tudor connection highly. No. 16 Cheyne Walk had a wrought-iron gateway incorporating the monogram 'CR'. Amateur history buffs thought the initials stood for Caterina Regina and referred to Katherine Parr. When it was proved that the gate was of a later design someone assumed Charles II's wife, Catherine of Braganza, had lived there, but the Katherine Parr faction were adamant. They found Tudor brickwork and argued passionately that No. 16 was on the site of the Old Manor. Catherine of Braganza's supporters included the Revd and Mrs Haweis, who moved to No. 16 in 1882. Mrs Haweis was so convinced that Catherine had spent long, lonely nights there while the King misbehaved with that 'frail woman' Nell Gwynn further down the river at Sandford

Manor, that she renamed her premises 'Queen's House'. The Revd Haweis grandly declared the cellars 'of the Hampton Court period'. At this point the great architectural sleuth Mr Randall Davies spoiled things by observing that the house was not built until 1717 – twenty-five years after Catherine of Braganza had returned to Portugal. The initials on the gate were those of Richard Chapman, a wealthy apothecary, who was the first tenant.

Before this discovery, however, the Katherine Parr theory held such romantic appeal that, in 1862, when Rossetti moved to No. 16 with his menagerie, his friends and his models, the mansion was called Tudor House. The painter furnished it with suitable antiques ranging from massive oak panels to a four-poster bed with embroidered curtains. Here the Pre-Raphaelite Brotherhood met and painted, drank and feasted, until they embarked on their downward spiral. Millais and Holman Hunt had already gone their separate ways, but Dante Gabriel was visited by Ruskin, William Morris, Burne-Jones and the poet Algernon Charles Swinburne, who was youthful and beautiful.

In summer Swinburne showed off. He would walk about naked, upsetting the servants, though he had not yet succumbed to that taste for flagellation which was to surface later in St John's Wood. Ruskin naïvely proposed himself as a member of the colourful household, but his lifestyle was not congenial to the others, so the offer was refused. He had gone through a seven-year marriage with Euphemia Chalmers-Gray which was so deeply spiritual that she divorced him for impotence. The gossips claimed that as Greek sculptors all portrayed women after depilation, when the great man saw Euphemia undressed for the first time on their wedding night, he assumed her to be uniquely disfigured by pubic hair. She became Lady Millais, while Ruskin confined himself to presenting signed copies of *Sesame and Lilies* to the maiden chosen annually as Chelsea's May Queen.

Rossetti's appetites were more straightforward and his artistic and sexual needs coincided felicitously. He married

Elizabeth Siddal, a milliner's apprentice with a mass of red-gold hair who was his model for ten years. Eight months before the painter came to Cheyne Walk, however, 'Lizzie' died of an overdose of laudanum. She was found unconscious with the empty bottle beside her, having tried to cure a migraine. Rossetti then took as his housekeeper Fanny Cornforth, a buxom cockney girl from Wapping with a cascade of golden hair, who was also an excellent cook. For propriety's sake, she lived at 36 Royal Avenue, but spent most of her time at Cheyne Walk, producing superb meals and dropping her aitches. She was Rossetti's mistress for sixteen years, until she developed middle-aged spread, whereupon he nicknamed her 'the Elephant'. Simultaneously he was passionately in love with William Morris's wife, Jane, the model for his sulkily voluptuous Proserpine. As the Elephant grew fatter, he took up with a younger model, Alexa Wilding, another red-haired beauty. Fanny extorted money from Rossetti until she married her lodger and went to manage a hotel in Jermyn Street.

Although Victorian Society could tolerate a little artistic bohemianism in men, it gave no quarter to fallen women. Mary Ann Evans assumed the pen name 'George Eliot' to overcome prejudice against women writers. She also flouted convention by living for twenty years with the essayist G. H. Lewes. They were accepted in artistic circles, but even her own brother would not speak to her. After the success of *The Mill on the Floss* and *Silas Marner*, however, even Queen Victoria became one of her admirers. In 1878 Lewes died and two years later Mary Ann married Walter Cross, her financial adviser. They went to live at No. 4 Cheyne Walk.

A sad little story, rarely told, is that after Mr and Mrs Cross settled into their meritorious address, the great novelist tried to play the part of a banker's wife. She lit the panelled room with many candles, arranged flowers and set out the finest food. The candles guttered, the food went cold. No guests came. It was a calculated snub by her respectable neighbours to indicate that the woman who had defied convention by living with Lewes could not now join their ranks simply by embarking upon Holy

Matrimony with Cross. Mary Ann and John took the food in baskets and gave it to the poor in Paradise Walk, which had deteriorated into a slum.

10
The Sex Goddess

Only one thing shocked Victorian Society more profoundly than behaviour like Mary Ann's: divorce. Separation was tolerated, but for a couple to air their differences in 'that well of defilement, that filthy pesthouse, the Divorce Court' spelled social ruin. When the Prince of Wales became engaged to the Danish Princess Alexandra, Queen Victoria wrangled with the Archbishop of Canterbury over wedding dates. The only day which suited all parties fell in Lent 1863 and the prelate objected. Weddings, he felt, should not be celebrated in that season of abstinence. The Queen, conscious of the dignity which Supreme Headship of the Established Church conferred, rounded on the unfortunate cleric. 'Marriage, Archbishop,' she said with authority, 'is a solemn and holy duty, not a pleasure to be taken lightly.' And that was the end of the matter.

When the wedding of twenty-three-year-old Gertrude Elizabeth Blood and Lord Colin Campbell, youngest son of the 8th Duke of Argyll took place at the Savoy Chapel in 1881, it had all the hallmarks of a happy union. The Queen's daughter Princess Louise was one of the guests. There were six brides-maids in lace and muslin with ribbons of Garter Blue; three clergymen, including the Queen's Chaplain, officiated; dukes and marquises attended the reception and the bride's relations, who were Anglo-Irish gentry, had come to an agreement with the groom's father about a jointure. The young couple would have £16,000 a year, not a fortune to be sure, but enough for them to keep four servants and set up house in Cadogan Place.

No one in Society dreamed that five years later the marriage would end in a notorious court case. The hearing lasted eighteen days. It was the longest and most sensational divorce trial in modern history. There were reports in more than forty newspapers. Lord Colin accused his wife of committing adultery with a Duke, a General and the Chief of the London Fire Brigade. She accused him of carrying on with a parlourmaid. At the last minute he added a doctor to the list of co-respondents. The defence lawyers claimed he was trying to avoid paying his medical bill.

The *Morning Post* had reported that the honeymoon would be spent in Switzerland. Erroneously, as it happened, for the Campbells spent their honeymoon at Ventnor in the Isle of Wight. Lord Colin's surgical nurse was in attendance and Lady Colin did not part with her virginity for many months. Educated at Eton and Cambridge, Lord Colin was a man of mediocre talents. He was also economical with the truth. As a result of indiscretions as an undergraduate he had contracted syphilis. Eleven different doctors had failed to find a cure. All this information he withheld from his beautiful, gifted and consummately educated wife, pretending that he needed a nurse because he had a fistula. Lord Colin was MP for his family's safe Liberal seat in Argyllshire. It was assumed that the young man would make a career for himself in politics. Instead, he became a semi-permanent invalid.

Some months after the wedding the couple went to stay amid the rolling acres of Argyll Castle and in this romantic setting the marriage was finally consummated. Lady Colin's introduction to conjugal bliss, however, was perfunctory. Lord Colin passed her a cutting from a surgeon's letter indicating that intercourse would improve his health. The following morning he advised her to take precautions against infection.

It was suggested at the trial that this was not the way 'a man of delicacy' should put such a matter to 'a young pure-minded wife'. Lady Colin was not only pure; like most young women of her time, she was hopelessly ignorant about sex. When she experienced searing pain as a result of Lord Colin's disease, she bore it loyally, assuming it to be part of a wife's natural suffering. After she did understand what had happened, she maintained a polite façade, went out in Society and was seen often at theatres and balls, chaperoned by her married sister Mrs Bolton and her fashionable cousin, Lady Miles.

Lady Colin had an extrovert personality. She sang at charity concerts, visited exhibitions and was acquainted with artists and musicians; James Whistler painted her in a white satin ballgown by Worth; at the first night of *Iolanthe*, she was in a party which included Sir Arthur Sullivan. Unpleasant duties, such as the changing of Lord Colin's dressing, she left to the nurse. When 79 Cadogan Place was fixed upon as the matrimonial home, Lady Colin supervised the decoration because Lord Colin was frequently confined to his sickroom. Unfortunately, before the premises were fully furnished, she received male visitors in the drawing-room. This caused her Swiss maid to gossip and set her manservant spying through the keyhole. He reported in court that he had seen Lady Colin lying down on the carpet with Captain Shaw. She had also been sighted *smoking a cigarette* with General Butler and speaking to her friend and neighbour the Duke of Marlborough's heir, Lord Blandford. Admittedly, this last was a serious indiscretion, for Lord Blandford was a notorious rake who had seduced Lady Aylesford, bringing about her complete social downfall and a separation from her husband.

The Campbell trial opened on 26 November 1886. Most of the evidence was servants' gossip of the lowest kind. Sensation followed sensation and the court was packed. Ladies were excluded on account of the loathsome nature of the evidence but, as the men accused of misbehaving with Lady Colin were of such eminence, their counsel were all stars of the legal profession. Young barristers flocked to hear the eight QCs conduct their cross-examinations.

Lord Blandford's father had recently died, so that he had become the Duke of Marlborough. He was represented by the Attorney-General, Sir Richard Webster, the highest advocate in the land, while Tom Bird, the doctor in the case, had engaged the second grandest lawyer, the Solicitor-General. When it transpired that Lady Colin had spoken to Lord Blandford while walking her collie dog in Cadogan Square, the Attorney-General made mincemeat out of the earnest policeman who had observed them. 'Are two people who have known each other for a considerable time', he asked incredulously, 'not to speak, or walk together in a *square*?'

On the first day of the trial the Duke of Argyll attended wearing a black morning coat relieved only by a gold watch chain. He left before it was revealed that his son had employed a private detective to trail Lady Colin to Paris in an attempt to get her arrested as a common prostitute. Even the judge considered this blackguardly. On the second day, Lady Colin's cousin Lady Miles entered the witness box in an elegant hat and a high, exquisitely ruffled lace collar. Campbell's counsel tried to confuse her about dates. A spirited society figure, she gave as good as she got but, seeing Robert Finlay the great Scottish QC put down, the junior barristers began clapping and the applause spread to the gallery. The whole court joined in the ovation. 'Silence,' thundered Judge Butt. 'I will not have clapping of hands. It is indecent in the extreme.' The court adjourned for the weekend.

The Sunday papers made the most of the story. Lady Colin had become a 'sex goddess'. There were calls for Whistler's painting of her, 'A Harmony in White and Ivory', to be withdrawn from the exhibition of the Society of British Artists. By Monday morning the Strand was filled with crowds. Inside the law courts the corridors were jammed. Wooden barriers had to be erected round the entrance to Court No 1. Amelia Watson, the parlourmaid whom Lord Colin was reputed to have seduced, had been examined by two doctors and pronounced a virgin. On the seventh day of the trial a rumour spread that Captain Shaw, the Chief of the London Fire Service and a man renowned throughout London for his heroism and probity, had committed suicide. The story was discredited when Captain Shaw, in robust good health, walked into the court and shook hands with Lady Colin and her mother.

More column space was given to *Campbell v. Campbell* than to world events. On the eleventh day of the trial a letter appeared in *The Times* complaining of the reporting. The writer wished the Editor could induce other newspapers to present the facts more rationally. 'I hear everywhere loud complaints as to the grave mischief caused by the details, which some journals think fit to give . . . and of the effect which these reports have on servants, on the young and on the working classes. Young lads devour the details as they go home from work. Servants sit up at night to read them.' It was a scandal, the writer said, that the Attorney-General and the Solicitor-General, officers of the Crown appearing in the case, could not prevent the stories 'turning to the corruption of a nation'.

The *Daily Telegraph* was the chief culprit. On the morning after the trial opened it had printed 1,395 lines. The *Liverpool Post* came a close second, while the *Evening Standard* and the *London Evening News* vied for full coverage, though even they deemed the details 'unfit for publication' when it came to the 'evidence' against Captain Shaw. Despite an outcry against prurience, all the papers continued to make daily reports and to enjoy record circulation. In Birmingham a pious reader praised the *Daily Gazette* for its restraint: 'I am relieved you have exercised discrimination in reporting the revolting Colin Campbell case . . . I am glad one newspaper has the courage to run counter to those depraved tastes which seemed to devour the most vicious details with the greatest relish.'

When the outcry against 'A Harmony in White and Ivory' threatened to disrupt the Society of Artists' show, Whistler, delighted by all the publicity, sent Lady Colin an encouraging note: 'You are of course Splendid. To be understood by you is my delight. To do beautiful things with you is my ambition.'

By the thirteenth day of the trial Mrs Blood and Lady Miles brought cushions into the courtroom. Together with Lady Colin and the female witnesses, they were the only women allowed into the arena. On the fourteenth day the Duke of Marlborough appeared. He was the very picture of savoir faire, but the affair with Lady Aylesford had ruined his character. Wicked and immoral the Duke might be, said the Attorney-General, but there was no rule in society that decreed he should therefore be ostracized.

The jury, meanwhile, had all visited 79 Cadogan Place to examine the celebrated keyhole through which O'Neill the butler had claimed to see Lady Colin stretched out on the floor with Captain Shaw. The Captain's word that the story was 'absolutely untrue from beginning to end' was accepted unequivocally, but General Butler, who was also one of the accused, declined to appear. As a practising Catholic, he had no wish to cross the threshold of a divorce court. He came in for heavy censure. On the last day of the trial, when the jury found both Lord Colin and Lady Colin innocent of the charges they had brought against each other, the Foreman requested permission to read out a statement: 'The jury desire to express an opinion that in not coming forward in the interests of justice, General Butler acted in a manner unworthy of an English officer and gentleman.'

The costs of the case were about £20,000, in those days an astronomical sum. The Duke of Argyll paid. Lord Colin went to Bombay. Lady Colin moved into Carlisle Mansions near Victoria Station, an address very different in tone from Cadogan Place. As a woman who had been dragged through the divorce court, she could no longer be received in society although, like George Eliot, she was accepted in literary and artistic circles.

Lady Colin went on to write for her living, contributing to the *Saturday Review*, the *Pall Mall Gazette* and the *World*. In 1889 she became art editor of the *World* for which she wrote a weekly column, 'In the Picture Galleries'. She used a pen name and she was among the best art critics of her day. She was also editor of the *Ladies' Field*, a magazine which dealt with 'whatever women did indoors and outdoors'. It was full of decorous advice about how to dress for the opera and what to wear for shooting-parties. Although she was forced by cruel circumstances to become one of the most emancipated women of her century, Lady Colin would never, even remotely, have considered herself a feminist.

11
Love Among the Artists

Whistler never did realize his ambition to 'do beautiful things' with Lady Colin but, a decade later, she was painted by Giovanni Boldini in the challenging pose on the jacket of this book. It was Boldini's delight to exaggerate and to make outrageous distortions in the interest of slimness and elegance. Whistler's pupil Walter Sickert called him the supreme exponent of the 'wriggle and chiffon school of portraiture'. Corsetry in the 1890s was going through a boom. The eighteen-inch waist was every woman's target. Ladies squeezed their intestines into whalebone cages of incredible dimensions to achieve the fashionable effect and there was much fainting if they suddenly drew breath. Boldini, with his unique ability to emphasize a curve, had a field day. He worked in Paris, where he occupied the studio formerly used by John Singer Sargent.

As the leading society portrait painter in London, Sargent was able to command astronomical fees and, having moved to Chelsea he succeeded in making 31 Tite Street the centre of fashion. Wholly solvent, he became so tired of being asked for small loans that he hung a basket of money in his hallway from which friends could take what they needed.

James McNeill Whistler, Jimmie to his friends, was also at the height of his fame. By the time of the Campbell trial, however, the dapper American had been ruined financially by his quarrel with Ruskin. This had cost him the White House, the superb studio which Edward Godwin had designed for him with its roof of green slate and windows placed where they would shed light, instead of for external symmetry. Inside, the walls were pure yellow, of an intense shade mixed especially by Whistler himself – as a foil for the blue and white china he liked to collect. Charles Augustus Howell, the flamboyant art-broker who told stories as unbelievable as Baron Munchausen's and who faked Rossetti's work so perfectly that no one could spot the originals, complained that staying with Jimmie was like 'living inside an egg'.

Whistler came to London in 1859 after a Bohemian phase studying in Paris. When he had absorbed everything the Left Bank could teach, he crossed the Channel, leaving behind his passionate gypsy mistress, Fumette. Jo Heffernan, a red-haired Irish beauty, was his new model. Whistler quickly gauged the sexual tempo of Victorian England and painted Jo as 'the Little White Girl', a demure study in which she holds a Japanese fan. Masquerading discreetly as his wife, she became his mistress, until the artist's mother came to London. The arrival of Mrs Whistler, a Massachusetts puritan, brought the idyll to an abrupt halt.

Whistler's etchings gained him immediate fame. He fell hopelessly in love with Chelsea and his Thames series disclosed a new vision of the river, recording for posterity barge and clipper, warehouse and waterside tavern. With his Nocturnes he was trying to do something new, which profoundly upset Ruskin who saw himself as the leader of the Artistic Establishment. Walter Greaves, the cockney boatman who became Whistler's pupil, recorded the elaborate preparations which went into a Nocturne. Walter and his brother Henry, the sons of a Thames boatbuilder, were at first mere assistants whom the painter tipped to carry his palette and easel. The American taught the brothers to paint and they taught him to row with a stroke called 'the waterman's jerk'. Walter and Henry would row Whistler past Cremorne Gardens, where the band played and the dancers whirled as magnificent fireworks shot into the sky. Night after night the artist would sit in the boat, sketching his Nocturne on brown paper with black and white chalk. He would then paint with very swift strokes for two days, working from the dozens of sketches, trying to capture the spirit of what he proprietorially called 'My Chelsea'. To Ruskin such a technique was incomprehensible.

In 1876 Whistler exhibited at the newly opened Grosvenor Gallery. The show included a portrait of Carlyle for which the Glasgow Art Gallery was eventually to pay 1,000 guineas. Carlyle himself was satisfied with the likeness which had taken many sittings. Ruskin ignored the portrait, but vented his spleen upon 'Nocturne in Black and Gold', a picture of a falling rocket, which was the culmination of many nights spent on the river. It was impudence, thundered Ruskin, 'for a coxcomb' to ask two hundred guineas 'for flinging a pot of paint in the public's face'.

Whistler was an American gentleman. He was nearly an officer too for, before the Bohemian phase in Paris, he spent a year at West Point, the élite military academy. He took Ruskin to court. The critic was too ill to appear, but he was represented by Sir Edward Burne-Jones and Tom Taylor, the Arts Correspondent of *The Times*. The affair began to assume all the excitement of a duel. Whistler's seconds were the artists Albert Moore and William Rossetti, brother of Dante. The Attorney-General conducted the questioning but the jury, who were not art critics, found much of the sparring above their heads. Whistler was awarded a farthing damages.

The legal costs were ruinous and he was forced to sell the White House before it was completed. It was a bad business for all concerned, especially for the architect Edward Godwin, who had fallen in love with Beatrice Phillips, the daughter of the sculptor responsible for the frieze on the Albert Hall. At this point the story takes an almost incestuous turn. Whistler went to live in Venice with his mistress, Maud Franklin – another red-head – but he could not bear the separation from his beloved Chelsea. By 1880 he was back in Tite Street in a rented studio, violently hating Tom Taylor who had bought the White House at a bargain price. The American artist was a superb self-publicist, attending the Fine Art Society exhibition with a cane in one hand, leading a beautiful white pomeranian dog on a long ribbon with the other and gazing at the work through his monocle. When Godwin died, Whistler married his widow, Beatrice, but to marry Beatrice, Godwin had deserted Ellen Terry, who owed quite a lot of her early success to the writings of Tom Taylor.

Meanwhile, the aesthetic craze which had been in its infancy when Whistler left for Venice had reached its height. It was enduringly satirized by W.S. Gilbert in *Patience*, first performed in 1881. Very soon the two greatest aesthetes in Chelsea were Whistler and a young man newly down from Oxford, who wore lavender gloves. His name was Oscar Wilde. Everyone believed Oscar to be the model for Bunthorne, the poet in *Patience*, who walked down Piccadilly 'with a poppy or a lily' in his medieval hand. He affected green velvet coats, knee breeches and flowing locks. Whistler and Wilde enjoyed bandying witticisms and their most famous exchange, though often quoted, is too good to let pass. After one of Whistler's sallies, Wilde, who had a reputation for stealing other people's jokes said, 'I wish I'd said that.' Whistler adjusted his monocle and replied, 'You will, Oscar, you will.'

Wilde soon went to live in Tite Street himself, partly because his mother, Lady Wilde, had recently moved from Mayfair to Oakley Street, but also because it was where he had once seen Ellen Terry on her way to Sargent's studio for a sitting. In the full light of day, the great actress stepped out of a four-wheeler, dressed unforgettably as Lady Macbeth. Her costume was green and blue, iridescent with beetles' wings. It had been created by Mrs Nettleship, the wardrobe lady at the Lyceum. Ellen though it 'one of Mrs Nettles' greatest triumphs' and was glad it would be 'immortalized in the Sargent portrait'. When the picture was exhibited it was the sensation of the year, attracting dense crowds day after day. Oscar's taste for flamboyant dress was shared by his mother, who presided over a crowded salon in Oakley Street, as the popular poetess 'Speranza'. At her receptions she would appear in flowing robes of purple velvet and crowned with a wreath of golden bay-leaves.

Ellen Terry once declared that the most remarkable men she had ever known were Whistler and Oscar Wilde. Both, she said, 'were more audacious than it is possible to describe'. By the standards of her day, Ellen Terry's own behaviour was fairly audacious, but she was the darling of the English theatre for over five decades and somehow she always escaped without a breath of censure. Ellen made her stage début in Charles Kean's company, when she was nine years old. As the daughter of two of Kean's players, Ben and Sarah, she was allowed to play Mamillius, the infant prince in *A Winter's Tale*. The first night was memorable. In front of an audience which included Queen Victoria, Prince Albert, the Princess Royal and a young man who would later become famous under the name of Lewis Carroll, she spoke her lines loudly and clearly. All went well until Leontes uttered the command 'Go play, Mamillius.' The young actress had been entrusted with a beautiful stage prop, a small cart made in exact replica of one on a Greek vase. She romped across the stage with boyish vigour but fell over the handle of her toy and landed on her back. It was the end, she felt, of her theatrical career, although she was hugged by Mrs Kean and continued to play Mamillius for one hundred and two nights.

Ellen grew into a stunning beauty. When she was sixteen she and her sister Kate sat for the painter G.F. Watts. Like most of her generation she knew nothing about sex. When Watts kissed her a shade too warmly, she assumed she would automatically have a baby, so she married him at St Barnabas Church, Kensington without further ado.

The marriage was not a success. Watts was forty-seven and inclined to take himself seriously. He lived at Little Holland House, now demolished, but then an imposing country mansion to the west of Holland House which, to Ellen, must have seemed as palatial as Holland House itself. There the important painter entertained grave and interesting friends, but his new wife, who was used to the cheerful, theatrical rough-and-tumble of her parents' household, failed to match up to the exacting standards of decorum thought desirable.

For a time Watts was besotted by her beauty. When she was seventeen he painted her with her red-gold hair rippling about her shoulders in 'Choosing', the study now in the National Portrait Gallery. For the Victorians the picture was heavy with symbolism. Ellen sniffs a scarlet camellia, the flower which signified unpretending excellence, but in her hand she crushes sweet violets, the emblem of modesty. Bored to tears by the restrictions imposed by Watts's draconian housekeeper, Mrs Prinseps, the young bride indulged in mischievous and unconventional behaviour. One night she appeared at dinner, dressed as Cupid in pink tights and a Grecian tunic. Watts was not amused. Eighteen months later he demanded a separation. Mortified, Mrs Watts was sent back to her parents, the loving Ben and Sarah. She felt an acute sense of failure.

Whistler's architect, Edward Godwin, was the great love of Ellen Terry's life and the father of her children, Edy and Gordon Craig. She left the stage and eloped with him to Hertfordshire where, for six years, they enjoyed a rustic idyll until he became attracted to Beatrice Phillips. One of Ellen's biographers called the actress, whom many remember as a grande dame, 'an exceedingly early hippy'. She used earthenware pots decades before they were the fashion and wore loose garments, including Japanese kimonos supplied by Whistler, who was one of the few London friends who knew her whereabouts.

Just before the Hertfordshire ménage broke up, Ellen was tempted back to the theatre. Out driving with her children in a pony cart, she heard the sound of a horn and a huntsman in a pink coat leaped over the hedge. He was Charles Reade, a friend from the past. Without dismounting, he reined in his horse crying 'Good God, it's Nelly'. There and then he asked her to take over the lead in *The Wandering Heir*, his successful production at the New Queen's theatre. Ellen thought of the bailiffs who were about to foreclose on Godwin and asked for forty pounds a week. She got it.

Watts finally gave Ellen a divorce and her second marriage

was to actor Charles Kelly who, predictably, took to drink when she began to outshine him. This was through her celebrated, though wholly professional partnership with Sir Henry Irving. She had by then long since acquired the social graces she had lacked as Mrs Watts and always acted as hostess at the wonderful parties Irving gave at the Lyceum. Ellen married Kelly when they were both playing at the Court Theatre in Sloane Square, later the Royal Court and in Ellen's time the birthplace of many of Shaw's early plays. Long after she had separated from Charles Kelly, she was summoned to his deathbed, where she was seized by an irrational desire to start rehearsing Juliet. Charles Reade, who knew her well, once described her as '*enfant gatée et enfant terrible*'.

None of her marriages lasted very long, but they broke up without too much scandal. Her third was to James Carew, a young American actor from Indiana, with whom she toured in Shaw's *Captain Brassbound's Conversion*. Ellen had just received the homage of a lifetime in a grand jubilee at Drury Lane to celebrate her fiftieth year in the theatre. Carew was in his thirties. Poor Edy, who had feminist tendencies, was terribly shocked by this display of maternal allure.

Three years before her marriage to Carew, Ellen had decided to make Chelsea her London home. Invisible threads seemed to draw her back. Perhaps she remembered the halcyon days, when Wilde has sent her great bunches of lilies to show his admiration. She had been greatly pleased by his sonnet comparing her to 'a wan lily', which was inspired by her memorable performance as Henrietta Maria in Irving's production of *Charles I*. When Oscar married and moved to Tite Street in 1884, the ubiquitous Godwin designed the interior of the house, creating for the Wildes an all-white dining room with curtains embroidered in yellow silk. It was startlingly avant-garde. Ellen Terry and Henry Irving were regular visitors and on the dreadful night when Wilde fled to his mother's house in Oakley Street, having been granted bail from Holloway Prison, a veiled lady brought him violets. The bearer of the bouquet probably did not understand the terrible nature of the crime of which Oscar stood accused, but the card which accompanied it demonstrated that Ellen Terry's friendship was unswerving. It said simply 'For Luck'.

12

The Jersey Lily and the Flame of Art

In Pont Street, that wonderfully straight thoroughfare which rises in Belgravia and runs through Upper Chelsea to the tip of Beauchamp Place, there is a blue plaque above what was once the front door of the Cadogan Hotel. It commemorates Lillie Langtry, the beautiful actress who became the mistress of the Prince of Wales, later King Edward VII. The Cadogan Hotel is also the meeting place for the annual dinner of the Oscar Wilde Society, but its front door has been moved round the corner into Sloane Street to accommodate the premises of Thomas Pink, appropriately named makers of flamboyant gentlemen's shirts.

Wilde only stayed one night at the Cadogan Hotel, but it was the scene of his arrest when, hounded by the press and a jeering London mob, he fled there after the collapse of his libel case against the Marquis of Queensberry. His career was in ruins. He dared not return to Tite Street, where his wife and children had learned of his defeat, but scarcely comprehended that he faced two years' imprisonment for offences against young men. Homosexuality was a crime ladies did not understand and a word too awful to be breathed in their presence. 'Poor Oscar,' wept the bewildered Constance, 'he must go abroad.' But she did not know why, only that her husband had done something which 'abroad' would not be considered so evidently dreadful.

Everyone thought that Oscar would flee to the Continent. Even the magistrate delayed signing the warrant to give him time to catch the boat train, but Wilde remained at the hotel, drinking hock and seltzer. He was drained of emotion and probably dazed with shock, though later, Lady Wilde and Oscar's alcoholic brother Willie, turned the delay into favourable publicity. 'Oscar is an Irish gentleman. He will stay to face the music.' It was Willie's finest line, uttered to all who called at Oakley Street and undoubtedly inspired by Speranza who, in a sudden burst of grand-maternal energy, packed off Constance and the children to endure 'abroad' as best they could.

In the 1880s Lillie Langtry and Oscar Wilde were twin stars in the same blazing firmament, but Oscar has had more publicity in our own times. Sir John Betjeman captured for ever the moment when the two constables knocked on the door of Room 53.

Mr Woilde, we 'ave come for to take yew
Where felons and criminals dwell
We must ask yew to leave with us quoietly
For this IS the Cadogan Hotel.

The poem goes on to tell how Oscar put down *The Yellow Book*, the avant-garde journal, which published drawings by Aubrey Beardsley and essays by Max Beerbohm. It approved 'Art for Art's Sake' and was generally considered a very scandalous publication. Oscar was not actually reading it at the time of his arrest; he was reading a book in a yellow cover, Pierre Louys' enduringly erotic novel, *Aphrodite*, but the papers wrote, 'Oscar Wilde Arrested. Yellow Book under his Arm'. An angry crowd gathered outside the Bodley Head office in Vigo Street and stoned the windows. Soon afterwards the publication ceased.

How surprised the Victorians would have been to learn that their fallen idol has become a hero of our time. How proud Lady Wilde to hear that the hundredth anniversary of her son's death is being marked by the Chelsea Society with a statue by Sir Eduardo Paolozzi, the most expensive sculptor in Europe. How

Whistler might have crowed if he had known it was to be sited at the World's End, and how Constance would have blushed if she could have foreseen that the bedroom where Oscar took refuge to spare her shame has been renovated, most tastefully, in a greenery-yallery William Morris print with curtains of real Nottingham lace, and is let as 'the Oscar Wilde Room' at £230 a night.

The Lillie Langtry suite is also being refurbished. The famous actress made 21 Pont Street her home in 1892, occupying five floors which have since become part of the Cadogan Hotel. The Prince of Wales's feathers, her leitmotif, are still visible on the ceilings, while her exquisite drawing-room is now the hotel's dining-room. It too has recently been redecorated – a harmony in peach, as Whistler would have said – with the listed plasterwork of musical instruments picked out in ivory, and the walls hung with Coalport in the shade of a dove's wing. Certainly Pont Street was the most tasteful of Lillie's homes, though it was not the luckiest. By the time she settled there she had been through many adventures and had amassed jewels worth a small fortune. They were kept in a tin box, two feel tall, which was deposited when Lillie was travelling at the Union Bank in Sloane Street. It contained sapphires from Tiffany's, a parure of emeralds and diamonds which had belonged to the Empress Eugènie, a brooch said to be set with the largest ruby in the world and a flashing diamond and pearl tiara, which she sometimes wore on stage. If interest was lacking, out would come the tiara to stun the audience back into attention. Although Lillie was a famous actress, her popularity did not always hinge on her histrionic abilities.

One morning it was discovered that the jewel box had been stolen. Mrs Langtry had been sailing in Cowes, but had stopped off in London for a few days as she wished to watch two horses of hers which were running. She sent her butler to the bank, where he was informed that the jewel box had been taken out on 18 August. The bank manager had written proof: Mrs Langtry had signed for it herself. Lillie was extremely proud of her pure complexion. She wore no make-up and had endorsed advertisements for Pears' Soap with her signature, which the thief had copied. Despite the offer of a large reward, and some keen detective work by Scotland Yard, the jewels were not found. Lillie sued the bank for negligence, but never recovered their full value.

She had first come to London in the spring of 1877 with two black dresses and a ballgown. Her father was the Dean of Jersey and she wore mourning for her brother Reginald, who had been killed in a riding accident. Her husband was in vigilant attendance. Mr Langtry derived a small income from property in Ireland, but it was not enough to sustain Lillie in the blaze of celebrity which was to follow her first London Season.

The young couple were invited to a party by Lady Sebright. Lillie's square-necked black dress, elegantly run up by the Jersey modiste, Madame Nicolle, showed off her shoulders to perfection. She wore no jewels because in those days she had none. Her hair was knotted in a bun, emphasizing her classical profile. It was the profile which was to be her undoing. On that first May evening in Society Sir John Millais took her in to dinner and asked if she would sit for him. 'I want to be the first to put your classic features on canvas,' he said. 'At supper Lady Sebright told her, 'You'll be the talk of London tomorrow.'

Very soon everything Lillie did was the talk of London. She had a talent for being talked about which was recognized and envied by the young Oscar Wilde. Invitations poured in but wherever Mrs Langtry went she continued to wear mourning for her brother, until one day Lady Dudley asked her to a ball, suggesting quite politely that she should not wear black because Lord Dudley had an aversion to it. That evening Mrs Langtry appeared in white velvet trimmed with pearls. As she entered the ballroom she was mobbed. People stood on chairs to get a glimpse of her. Photography had just become the fashion. Picture postcards of royalty, actresses and statesmen were on sale everywhere. Mrs Langtry's dress bills were driving Mr Langtry to drink. She sold her photographic rights to Downey's of Ebury Street and her face became more famous than ever. When she drove in the park, people lined the Row to get a glimpse of her celebrated profile.

Millais, who was also from Jersey, completed his portrait of her holding one of the island's native flowers, the Jersey Lily. She had hoped he would paint her classically draped, or in sumptuous medieval robes, but he insisted she should wear her black dress with a high, white lace collar. The only colour was the crimson flower in her hand. When the portrait was shown at the Royal Academy, it had to be roped off to keep back the crowds. George Smalley, art critic of *The Times*, praised her delicate colouring and curvaceous figure, adding 'yet the whole impression is one of vital force'. It was the 'vital force' which attracted the Prince of Wales and scandalized Queen Victoria. When Mrs Langtry was presented at Court, the Sovereign kept her eyes fixed on a point in the middle distance.

Oscar Wilde was twenty-two when Lillie began her first London Season. He had won the Newdigate Prize for Poetry at Oxford and he loved to be talked about. He could not afford bouquets, but he quickly realized that the importance of being Oscar would be enhanced by paying extravagant court to Mrs Langtry. He would buy a single lily or, if there were none available, a scarlet amaryllis, at Covent Garden and carry it as ostentatiously as possible to the Langtrys' lodgings in Norfolk Street. He wrote Lillie a sonnet, published in the *World*, which began: 'Lily of love, pure and inviolate'.

There is no record of what Mr Langtry, who had been married to her for three years, thought of this slur on his manhood. He devoted himself to fishing and losing at cards.

Oscar, meanwhile, tried to interest Lillie in Art but she remained chiefly fascinated by herself as a Work of Art. During her second London Season she was painted by Ellen Terry's first husband, G. F. Watts. Sir Edward Burne-Jones featured her twice in 'The Golden Stair' and Lord Leighton represented her as a shepherdess in 'Arcadia'. Whistler, more usefully, came round with a pot of gold paint and helped her improve her ceilings by covering them at small expense with gilded palm leaves. Oscar's friend Frank Miles drew a pencil sketch of her which was bought by Queen Victoria's youngest son, Prince Leopold, and hung above his bed at Buckingham Palace. When he was ill the

Queen went to visit him. She took one look at the picture, stood upon a chair and, there and then, took it down.

By this time Oscar had become terribly stage-struck. Long before the Prince of Wales made the suggestion, he told Lillie she should become an actress. He even tried to show her the first draft of a play he had written. Thinking it must be intended for drawing-room performance in Society, she asked him what her part was. 'A woman with a grown-up illegitimate daughter,' said Wilde. 'My dear Oscar,' she replied, 'am I old enough to have a grown up daughter?' She was twenty-seven and she would not even let him read it aloud to her. The play, *Lady Windermere's Fan*, was not produced until 1892, but it was horribly prophetic.

Years later, when Lillie was performing in America in Tom Taylor's play, *An Unequal Match*, the *New York World* invited Oscar to be guest critic. Unable to praise her acting, which was wooden, he raved for several paragraphs about her matchless beauty, filling the rest of the review with an essay on Greek art, a diatribe against scene painters and a joke about Whistler. Lillie's richest lover was Freddie Gebhard, the American multi-millionaire, who gave her a 6,500-acre ranch complete with bloodstock and real cowboys and Indians. He also contributed a private train with a silver bath, a piano fixed to the floor and rose silk curtains. Freddie would like to have married her, but he objected to her continuing friendship with the Prince of Wales, while his family jibbed at the fact that she was still married to Mr Langtry. When the poor man died in a Cheshire lunatic asylum she was free to marry Hugo de Bathe, the heir to a baronetcy.

As Lady de Bathe, which she became on her father-in-law's death in 1907, she was seen quite often in the south of France with her 'niece', Jeanne-Marie, who always supposed herself to be the daughter of Mr Langtry, or in a 'best case scenario', the bastard of the Prince of Wales. It was not until the eve of her own wedding to a staid Scottish chieftain, that Jeanne-Marie was tactlessly informed by Margot Asquith that her true father was Prince Louis of Battenberg. When Jeanne-Marie burst into tears of shock, Mrs Asquith said, 'Oh my dear, I thought you knew.'

13
Great Decorators

Sybil Colefax became a professional decorator when she was sixty-two after enjoying sixteen years of fame as one of London's leading hostesses. Hers was a radiant nature; she collected friends as some people collect antiques or rare books and she was noted for giving parties at which celebrities of the day mingled with politicians and statesmen. Widely satirized as a 'lion hunter', Sybil was the confidante of Mrs Simpson shortly before the Abdication Crisis. This social triumph raised her status far above that of Lady Cunard, her most serious rival, and threw her into paroxysms of worry about whether to inform the Prime Minister. Noël Coward, Aldous Huxley, the Windsors and H. G. Wells were just a few of the 'names' who enjoyed her charming hospitality. Enemies claimed that she was a social climber. In Chelsea if the wind blew until the shutters rattled, so that people said, 'What's that noise?' a popular joke was, 'Only the rungs of the ladder. It must be Lady Colefax out climbing.'

Sybil's childhood was spent shuttling between Cawnpore, Simla and Wimbledon. She married Arthur Colefax in July 1901, largely to escape her parents, and the couple set up house in Onslow Square, where Sybil arranged a memorable poetry reading, featuring T. S. Eliot and a pride of Sitwells. By all accounts it was a success but the hostess may have gushed too much, because Osbert took against her and joined the satirists. When she gave parties in Chelsea, he would lean out of the back window of the Sitwells' house in Carlyle Square and whenever a portentous guest raised Sybil's door-knocker bawl through a megaphone: 'And now comes the Swedish Ambassador.'

. . . and now comes the Swedish Ambassador.

As well as Onslow Square the Colefaxes had acquired Old Buckhurst, a Tudor manor in Sussex. After a brief period as Liberal MP for Manchester, Arthur took silk, having earlier been called to the Bar. A member of both the Athenaeum and the Garrick Club, he cannot have been as dull as Sybil's clever friends alleged. Maurice Bowra and Kenneth Clark were particularly beastly about him. Bowra had a private game drawing up imaginary cricket elevens of bores and they were always captained by Arthur Colefax. He was knighted in 1920 for services in the First World War. In the slump which followed, both Old Buckhurst and Onslow Square had to go, which is how the Colefaxes came to take Argyll House, the enchanting property at 211 King's Road built by Giacomo Leoni in the reign of George I. It took its name from the fourth Duke of Argyll, who had lived there in 1769.

When Leoni, who was a protegé of Lord Burlington, designed the house he wrote on the plans:

> Upon the King's Road between Chelsea and London this little house of my own Invention was built for Mr John Pirene ... the Apartments are of a size suitable for a private family. The Door in front is Doric with two columns, the Windows stone; the rest is grey brick which, in my opinion, sorting well with white stone, makes a beautiful Harmony of colours.

By the time Sybil and Arthur came upon Leoni's 'country house', Oakley Street had acquired several mansion blocks to the west and two terraced houses were joined on to the east in mellow red brick. Over the years they were tenanted by a number of celebrities and Sybil narrowly missed having Ellen Terry as a neighbour. The great actress moved from 215 King's Road only twelve months before the Colefaxes arrived (Sybil collected her regardless), but Argyll House with its great vine growing up the façade and a tangle of jasmine about the windows, certainly felt as though it was still in the country. Even today, when it faces the unlovely prospect of Chelsea Fire

Station, a holly bush and a silver birch tree grow in its tiny fore-court.

Sybil fell instantly in love with the house. It belonged at the time, to a Dr Thorne, who had practised there for over forty years, numbering Thomas Carlyle and Ellen Terry among his patients. Ellen, by then Dame Ellen, loved to relate in thrilling tones how she had once seen Carlyle, a stooping old man, coming down the doctor's stairs. Eventually Thorne retired and the Colefaxes moved in, modernizing, enhancing, improving. The dining-room was stripped of nine coats of paint to get back to the original panelling, which was 'the colour of a beechwood in October'.

Lady Colefax liked to keep everyone happy. She transformed the stables into servants' quarters where her staff could gaze out over the garden, but while the work was in progress she noticed that Leoni had not used grey brick at all, but yellow. When the Italian wrote the note on the plans, he must have confused the translation for the Italian words 'grigio' and 'giallo'. Sybil was a perfectionist about restoration. The stables were promptly remodelled in yellow brick of the exact type used by the archi-tect two hundred years earlier. It looked extremely nasty and caused an outcry from passing aesthetes walking down Oakley Street, but Sybil had not finished. When the bricklayers left, decorators zealously dirtied everything down again to an elegant grey with soot-blackened water.

Between the wars professional decorating was still in its infancy in England. To be properly British demanded a great deal of cream paint, and a touch of Adam green. Among the upper classes, hit by crippling death duties, it was widely held that a little shabbiness was no bad thing. Next door to Sybil at 213 King's Road, however, lived Syrie Maugham whose marriage to Somerset had been cruelly interrupted by his passionate homosexual love for Gerald Haxton. She sublimated her woe by rampaging across two continents decorating with breathtaking modernity. In 1922 she set up a shop in Baker Street, Syrie Limited, which soon expanded to grander premises in Mayfair.

The official leader of modern taste was Sir Charles White

Allom, who had designed the interior of the *Queen Mary*, as well as a great many swimming pools. He was much admired, but his imitators did not always have his sure touch. As a result a number of houses in the Home Counties acquired dining rooms like ocean liners. Lady Mendl, formerly Elsie de Wolfe, a lesbian and the apostle of florid chintz, had also set up in business after decorating the Colony Club in New York. Syrie, after a few experiments with flower prints, launched her celebrated all-white interiors. They caught on. All over London colour gave way to dazzling expanses of light and space. There was enough whiteness in Mayfair alone to bring on an epidemic of snow-blindness. *Vogue* heralded a 'Design Revolution' and, as husbands forked out to pay Syrie's bills, they muttered among themselves that she was God's gift to the dry-cleaning industry.

In the years before the Wall Street crash, Syrie Inc., the American side of her business, went from strength to strength. Elizabeth Arden introduced her to rich and influential friends. In Hollywood Mary Pickford opted for an all-white apartment. In Chicago the shop walls were hung entirely in raw silk. One day John D. Rockefeller's daughter, Mrs McCormick, walked in, impressively followed by her bodyguard. Syrie's right-hand man in America, John Neal, remembers the fabulously rich Mrs Edlinger querying the prices. 'If you don't have $10,000 to spend,' Syrie snapped, 'I don't want to waste my time talking to you.'

When the Wall Street crash did come and American clients defaulted over their bills, she had to close down the Mayfair showroom and shrink her empire. Ironically, she returned to Chelsea to open premises in Paradise Walk. As one of her American colleagues said, 'If she walked through a door, you would think, ''What a gracious lady'', but underneath was a superstructure of steel.'

Sybil turned professional in the early 1930s. Arthur by then was growing deaf and his practice at the Bar declined accordingly, so Sybil gallantly set herself the task of earning a £2,000 shortfall in the housekeeping. She opened an office at 24 Bruton Street in a corner of Stair & Andrew, the transatlantic antique dealers. Her style was in direct opposition to Syrie's. It shed the same rosy glow as her entertaining. Cecil Beaton said that she had decorated Argyll House 'with all the restraint of an eighteenth-century intellectual' using 'off colours – pale almond green, greys, opaque yellows and overall discretion.' When she worked professionally he was disappointed. He thought her rooms were unexceptional. The key to her style was a homely informality. 'Furnish your rooms for conversation' ran one of her maxims 'and the chairs will take care of themselves.'

As few hostesses have shared Sybil's capacity for lion-hunting, Beaton was bound to feel a sense of anti-climax, when he saw what she did for her clients. No amount of perfectly placed chairs could substitute for a party which included Diana Cooper, Noël Coward, the Duchess of Buccleuch and the King of England. Those were the guests invited on a memorable evening at Argyll House shortly before the Abdication Crisis reached its peak. George V had died; Edward VIII was uncrowned. Lady Colefax in imitation of Lady Cunard who would sometimes ask Richard Strauss to play, invited Artur Rubinstein to sit at the piano. Everyone went on talking including the King. The great musician glowered. The Princesse de Polignac, a genuine patron of music, visiting from Paris looked astounded. She had never encountered such rudeness. Sybil was almost in tears. The evening would have been a complete disaster had not Noël Coward taken over and played 'Mad Dogs and Englishmen' until hilarity was restored.

Next door at No 213, the guests shone not in the drawing-room but the ballroom, where the Bright Young Things danced the Charleston until dawn. Syrie's guest list could not compete with Sybil's, but it glittered nevertheless. While the King dined at 211, his younger brother, the Duke of Kent, danced at 213. Fancy dress was popular. On one occasion Syrie threw an all-white party, but no one warned the Duke. He came on from a night club in evening dress, a lone figure fox-trotting in sombre black. Maugham remained unimpressed. He was a terrible snob and considered Syrie had lowered herself by 'going into trade'.

In 1938 Sybil took on John Fowler, a young furniture restorer, who had a workshop at 292 King's Road. Both the great decorators adored him. Sybil's requirements were usually straightforward: a chair might need mending but Syrie had succumbed to the craze for painted furniture. Fowler worked for Peter Jones and had just supplied Lady Diana Cooper with a white-painted piano covered in crochets and semi-quavers. Syrie spotted a chance to get even with the American Customs, who charged outrageous taxes on antiques. She cheated shamelessly, overpainting priceless Chippendale chairs to get them passed as 'modern'. Some of her clients preferred Fowler's work to the originals and sometimes even the experts could not distinguish a genuine antique from a copy. Mrs Maugham loved bamboozling them. Pieces she commissioned still turn up from time to time on the *Antiques Road Show* – a tease for the cognoscenti.

Fowler was a brilliant artist, but not an astute businessman. Lady Colefax took him under her sociable wing. Suddenly he found himself dealing with some of the grandest clients in England and, through Sybil's astonishing network of friends, the celebrated Colefax & Fowler country-house style evolved. Detractors said that the secret of their success was to cover everything with patterns, so that no one would notice the dog hairs. Comfort with grandeur was the hallmark, until the outbreak of war limited their operations. During the Blitz customers flocked to them for blackout curtains and when there was no fabric available, Colefaxes dyed table-cloths to oblige.

Fortnum & Mason took over Syrie's shop in Paradise Walk, until it was wiped out by a German bomb, but Colefax & Fowler survived. Sybil eventually sold out to Nancy Lancaster, then Mrs Ronald Tree, but as Lady Colefax she remained socially indefatigable, using the shop every day to make telephone calls and write letters, even though it no longer belonged to her. No one minded: a stream of illustrious customers, often with bomb-damaged houses, continued to call at Bruton Street looking for Sybil. After the war the business expanded to include the

Fulham Road branch, so that it looped back to the place where it had begun – Chelsea.

Sybil was in her seventies when the war ended, but continued to give parties until the end of the decade, submitting to a nursing home only in 1950. Visitors still poured in. Terence Rattigan tried to hire an ambulance to take her to a play she wanted to see in Stratford. James Lee-Milne called to find T. S. Eliot sitting at the bedside and when Beverley Nichols visited one afternoon, Sybil was earnestly discussing *The Little Hut*, the play which had just taken London by storm, with its author, her 'newest young person', Nancy Mitford.

When the doctors could do no more, they took Sybil back to the house which had been her home since 1936, when Virginia Woolf had helped her pack up the last belongings from Argyll House, after Arthur's death. Harold Nicolson went to visit her, but he was just a few hours too late. The maid told him that on 21 September, the evening before she died, she had kept hearing Arthur knock at the door. She had asked the staff to let him in.

14
The Chelsea Set

During the war Chelsea was badly bombed. The German planes would fly up the Thames in search of Battersea Power Station, which was successfully camouflaged, but one landmark stood out, the Water Tower on Campden Hill in Kensington. As soon as the German pilots sighted it, they knew they had flown too far. They would do a U-turn, jettisoning spare bombs over Knightsbridge and Chelsea in hope of a random hit. The Old Church was almost completely destroyed. Only the More Chapel was left standing - a miracle, which reinforced Catholic determination to have him declared a Saint.

Many studios were damaged. Joan Wyndham woke one morning to learn that Redcliffe Road had been practically eradicated. She rushed round to find her friend Leonard's studio 'completely gone'. Two flights of stairs led up to doors that 'opened onto nowhere' and a bed upon which she had recently been deflowered was 'hanging out over the street'. Her girlfriend's gum tree was wedged upside down with its leaves moving gently in the breeze. Later the bed's occupant turned up to camp with her, carrying a guitar, a ginger cat called Henry Miller and a gas mask, inscribed, 'Rupert Charles Austin Darrow, still living by the grace of his own ingenuity'. Tite Street and Glebe Place remained standing, but by 1949, surveying the wreckage of the 'artists' quarter', Sir Gerald Kelly, the dynamic President of the Royal Academy boomed optimistically 'when you pull down one studio, build two.'

About thirty-four new studios were built after the War, mostly light, airy spaces at the top of tall blocks of flats, but in the early fifties Chelsea was a dingy, unfashionable place to live. In Bramerton Street a man bought two houses in which to keep hens. Fresh eggs were still in short supply. Property was cheap, but run down and undesirable. Entertainment consisted of evenings in pubs, followed by some very boozy bottle parties. Uninvited guests were welcome and would tag along when word went round a few minutes before closing time, where the scene would be. Algerian wine, tasting vaguely of turps, made its debut.

Chelsea, however, boasted three superb cinemas - the Essoldo, the Classic and the Paris Pullman, which drew in the post-war intelligentsia. At the Royal Court George Devine launched John Osborne and the 'Angry Young Men', but in the day-time the young resorted to the Kenco Coffee Bar and the Picasso Café, both thought avant-garde and a little bit decadent. A few ex-debutantes, in particular Lady Jane Vane-Tempest-Stewart and Sara Rothschild, strayed from Belgravia. Lady Antonia Pakenham was freshly down from Oxford and in 1957 Suna Portman and Mark Sykes appeared. Writing a decade later in *Harpers & Queen*, Anthony Haden Guest remembered that at all the best parties 'Michael Alexander showed up to woo dim-witted girls, whom he told he loved for their minds alone.'

In retrospect the antics of the set were dull beside those of their parents. At least the Bright Young Things had danced the Charleston, listened to jazz, squirted soda syphons and deprived policemen of their helmets. These young people dressed in sweaters, drank frothy coffee and discussed Sartre. They appeared to have nothing to do. In the West End the lighter side of fifties culture included *Salad Days*, the story of a magic piano which set people dancing. Enraptured audiences responded nightly to Julian Slade's trio sung by the hero's parents and his Aunt Prue, 'Find yourself something to do, dear. Find yourself something to do.' Slade, a *contented* young man, had hit on precisely the right vein of satire. The show ran for five years. It was the longest-running musical of its time. The author still banks royalties and when others are re-trenching has bought himself a flat in Beaufort Street.

Those whom the press named as leaders of the Chelsea Set have always denied that it existed. It was, they say, a figment of the gossip columns, but in 1959 the *Sunday Times* in those days a serious newspaper, published a feature complete with pictures of the young attending parties in garrets, or pretending to paint. Johnnie Moynihan of the *Evening Standard* was the chief chronicler of the set. One theory is that he used the phrase, 'a member of the Chelsea Set' to fill column space, much in the way he might have written 'Mayfair clubman' or 'Belgravia hostess'.

Things reached a climax when Edward Langley abducted an heiress, who tried to commit suicide after her parents succeeded in getting her made a Ward of Court. The *Evening Standard* got Michael Alexander to comment. In a sternly worded reproof he distanced himself and the party-goers of the early fifties from 'the Unsavoury Set - those semi-delinquent layabouts and their female hangers-on' who had turned the King's Road into 'not so much a hothouse as a jungle'. They could not, he said, claim even to be beatniks. They were unintellectual and their ethics were non-existent. Still branded as 'a Leader of the Chelsea Set' Michael had gone into the restaurant business. He was the first entrepreneur to appreciate the possibilities of Lot's Road. He opened up a café called the Gas Works near the World's End. Joan Wyndham was the cook and, glamorous in black satin, April Ashley, London's most celebrated sex-change patient, was the principal waitress.

Each decade has had its own 'Chelsea Set'. April's career spanned several. She ran her own restaurant, presiding nightly among the guests looking wonderfully regal. Like many cross-dressers, her profile was always enhanced by a tiara. During the fifties Prince Philip stopped the débutante presentations at Buckingham Palace. Many tiaras were stored in banks and family safe deposits, but the parties swung on. My own favourite was in Cheyne Walk in the early days of disco dancing. So much dry ice went into the special effects that the Chelsea Fire Station was alerted to smoke billowing from the windows. They sent four appliances to quell the conflagration. As Debdom refused to die, tiaras made their reappearance. The Denton girls inherited a share in one which came down from a Scottish bank by train with its own guard. When the aunt who left it to them died she added her house in St Luke's Street to the bequest. Her nieces found a shoe box in one of the cupboards labelled nonchalantly 'Spare rubies and diamonds'.

15
Models

Chelsea is probably the last place in the world, where the word 'model' does not conjure an image of a tall and slender blonde, groomed for *Hello!* magazine - a sound-bite crisply on her lips to the effect that she will not get out of bed for under £10,000 a day. Nor, in Chelsea, does the word 'model' signify that a girl has the sort of working background which would be implicit if it was written above a doorbell in Soho. Where the word is misused – in the literature which abounds so freely in our metropolitan telephone boxes – the numbers given are rarely for addresses in SW3. Chelsea is refreshingly free from sleaze. Here 'model' means a selfless person of either sex who is prepared to sit for many hours, clothed or unclothed, in the cause of Art.

The late Quentin Crisp once worked as a model. Shortly before his death he was very proud to be in an exhibition called 'The Artist's Model: from Etty to Spencer'. It was held at Kenwood House in Hampstead and gave Quentin a sense of belonging to the Establishment which he had so often lampooned. In his youth he courted attention but when fantastic garb became the norm in Chelsea he was rather sad. Francis King remembers that as a child he was walking along Fulham Road with his mother and sister. 'Suddenly an incredible figure walked towards us, dressed all in flowing silk scarves – a man wearing make-up and covered with flashing jewels. It was Quentin Crisp, who in those days lived in Beaufort Street. We had never seen anything like it. My mother hurried us past. "Don't stare," she said. "It only encourages them." But I kept wanting to turn round.' When Francis was a distinguished novelist in his own right, he told the story to Crisp. The author of *The Naked Civil Servant* delivered his epitaph on the shameless male exhibitionism which he now saw all about him: 'Ah, dear boy, if only they *would* turn round and stare.'

In modern times female models are on the whole commoner than male. There is no logical explanation for this. To analyse the whys and wherefores would be to enter the troubled zone of gender politics. In the days of the Pre-Raphaelite Brotherhood, models identified themselves with the painter's muse. Rossetti's obsession with William Morris's wife, Jane, is a case in point. In times when women had not cast off their traditional roles, painters were also a macho breed. Women were not admitted to the Chelsea Arts Club as members until 1966, when it was thought that the all-male preserve should try to bring itself more into line with the mores of the second half of the twentieth century. Even then, according to the club's historian, Tom Cross, it was thought that to allow women full membership 'might bring about cases of heart failure'.

Modelling for a life class is highly professional work. After tax it brings in a little less per hour than is asked by an average London cleaning lady. The art schools only employ people with a bona fide NHS number since the days when several schools were besieged by a Brazilian mafia of both sexes. Brazilians are keenly into the body beautiful and in general they sit with grace and poise. They are entitled to Portuguese passports, but are not eligible for European work permits. Heads of department found this difficult to explain, especially if confronted by a beguiling Brazilian who, speaking no English, was determined to make her good intentions understood by the simple operation of taking her clothes off. In the end, one harassed administrator had to issue his staff with a memorandum on how to identify a Brazilian, to prevent differences of opinion with the Home Office.

The traditional way to seek work is still for models to ring round the schools to ask if they are needed. At the Chelsea College of Art, which sprawls across four sites, each department

'Dear boy, if only they would *turn round and stare'*

has its own list of accredited models. The work is tough, involving sitting in the same posture clothed or unclothed for twenty to forty minutes at a time, but studio models still tend to build up a very special relationship with the artist. Stories abound of artists and their models but few perhaps have gone to such extremes as Oloff de Wet, the sculptor who made the superb bronze of Dylan Thomas in the Royal Festival Hall.

At the time of the Spanish Civil War de Wet, like many young Englishmen, decided to fight for the Communists. While he was waiting to enrol in a café at the foot of the Pyrenees, he began sketching a young waitress who told him that the Communists had captured her brother. One of the party members was rude to her and de Wet, never slow to defend a lady's honour, became involved in a brawl. When the moment to join the Spanish Army arrived, he signed up for the Fascists instead, because the other side had such bad manners. Asked after the conflict why he had done such a thing, de Wet kissed the tips of his fingers. 'She was so beautiful,' he said. 'How could I have done otherwise?'

In the 1950s the fees for clothed and unclothed models varied considerably. Henrietta Moraes, who was a Muse for Lucian Freud and a model for Francis Bacon, left a lucid account of why she posed. After a war-time childhood, during which she was thrashed by a sadistic grandmother and educated by a succession of fierce nuns, she was sent to Queen Anne's School, Caversham, where she had a crush on an older girl who kept the poems of T. S. Eliot under her pillow. Valerie Fletcher, the object of her passion, became Eliot's secretary. She later married him. 'Proof', said Henrietta, 'of a dedicated life.' In the post-war generation this was a fairly typical employment pattern.

Henrietta herself longed to be an actress. She confided in her Aunt Jo, who unquestioningly sent her to Queen's Secretarial College in South Kensington. She lived in bedsitter-land in Roland Gardens and her first secretarial job was with Eyre and Spottiswoode, publishers of the Bible, but Henrietta's heart was not in the typing pool. One morning she walked out of the office and rang all the art schools, asking for work as a model. On discovering that there were two types of modelling, 'Figure' and 'Head', and that the pay was respectively five shillings an hour and two and sixpence, she chose 'Figure'. Henrietta worked regularly, posing at Camberwell Art School, Heatherley's and Chelsea Art School in Manresa Road.

An habituée of jazz clubs, she lived for a time in Soho with film director Michael Law in an attic leased from Augustus John's daughter, Zoe. This was in the era when the Gargoyle Club still flourished and boasted such luminaries as Cyril Connolly, Brian Howard and Lucian Freud. Freud was the second love of Henrietta's young life. She was his model and mistress until she discovered a gruesome infidelity. At that point she married Michael Law, but the Bohemian life still called and she left him for a bi-sexual body-builder, Norman Bowler. This greatly upset Norman's friend Johnny Minton, a teacher at Chelsea College of Art, who was a great champion of representational painting and the talented illustrator of Elizabeth David's *Book of Mediterranean Food.*

After some cheerless years in Islington, Henrietta wrote: 'I never did like North London, even Notting Hill Gate seemed a strange country to me. I loved the River . . . I am drawn magnetically to it and most powerfully to the stretch between the end of Chelsea Embankment to Turner's Reach.' By a quirk of fate, Henrietta's disenchantment with 'north London' coincided with the discovery that Norman was having an affair with her best friend, while Johnny Minton chose that moment to die from a tragic overdose of barbiturates. He left Henrietta his beautiful studio at no. 9 Apollo Place, off Cheyne Walk. All 'rafters and beams', it looked out onto a walled garden full of magnolias, roses, lilies of the valley and bay trees. There she lived with her two children and later with Dom Moraes, the Indian poet, who had just won the Hawthornden Prize. They married at Chelsea Register Office in 1961 and lived happily until the day Dom went out to buy a packet of cigarettes and never came back.

As artists grew more Bohemian, so did the models.

Henrietta went on to be immortalized, though not always recognizably so, by Francis Bacon. The debate about representational and non-representational art still waxed hot, but Bacon's way of working included a minute study of form. He commissioned the photographer John Deakin to take dozens of pictures of Henrietta from every angle. Back in his studio Bacon would look at the shots, distorting them into his own unique artistic vision, which Philistines have occasionally compared to a plate of ham and eggs. Now, according to strict academic theory, the depiction of the naked figure should be 'a pure study unrelated to the erotic or personal proclivities of artist or model', but that is not always how nudes strike the untutored viewer. Henrietta one day walked into a pub and found Deakin flogging off redundant 'exposures' of their session to a fascinated crowd of naval ratings.

For a figure model the boundary between the professional and the personal is often a fragile one, but word gets round and models quickly learn which painters to avoid. Between the wars, Augustus John, a striking figure with his goatee beard, felt hats and brightly coloured bandannas, was noted for certain priapic tendencies. A hell-raiser who enthusiastically embraced the doctrine of free love, he married first Ida Nettleship, who gave him five children and later Dorelia, his model and mistress, by whom he had another four. As a student at the Slade, he had made friends with Francis Macnamara, an Irish poet and landowner. When their father left them, the Macnamara children were brought up with the young Johns at Alderney Manor in Dorset. Augustus himself veered between Chelsea, where he established a studio in Mallord Street, and various large country houses in Ireland, Dorset and Wales. Nicolette Macnamara adopted him joyfully as a second father, when she was six years old. She understood him with a rare sweetness. 'His living', she said, 'was an extension of his talent, an overflow of creativeness, a superabundance of the ''life force''. His sensuality ignored inhibition. In practice he did what he wanted to do and to hell with the neighbours.'

Not everyone viewed John with such indulgence. One evening at the Chelsea Arts Club there was almost a duel when Augustus kissed the hand of a lady who was escorted by Jacob Epstein. Construing the gesture as 'a pass', Epstein shouted, 'I will pull your bloody beard out.' Both parties were known to be fierce fighters and only the club steward's intervention averted disaster. He propelled Epstein through the door and shut it tight.

Dorelia, John's second wife, was known as Dodo. She and her sister Edie modelled for John and also provided a wardrobe for the shifting population of the household. All the children were expected to act as sitters and he liked them dressed in paintable fabrics which caught the light. The Johns and Macnamaras wore clothes which made them stand out painfully from other children: the boys had long belted smocks over corduroy trousers; the women and girls long flowing peasant dresses and loose tops in fabrics like velveteen and brightly dyed shantung. At the Carlton Hotel in Cannes the manager once refused them admittance, thinking them gypsies. He was apologetic when he saw the money-bag Augustus carried. The only surprising part of the story is that the painter didn't knock him down.

When he was in London John's thirst for beauty never abated. He was always on the look-out for models and sitters, and would be seen nightly in the Pheasantry 'talent-spotting'. In the decades after the war, poets and painters mingled freely in Chelsea. Nicolette Macnamara's sister Caitlin married Dylan Thomas and they lived for a time in Markham Square. Laurie Lee and Dylan Thomas were regular drinkers at the Queen's Elm. They were often joined by one of John's favourite models, the diminutive Diana. She was a tiny woman with wide, sparkling eyes. The two poets always offered Diana a seat, but wondered why she preferred to remain standing until one day she confided her secret. She was just small enough to slip under the counter when the barman wasn't looking. Once behind the bar, she would steal pieces of cheese.

In 1940 Augustus's grandest sitter was the present Queen Mother, who was then the Queen. Her Majesty sat patiently day after day, in the yellow drawing room at Buckingham Palace, wearing an evening dress embroidered with sequins. On one occasion she invited Augustus's patron, Hugo Pitman, to the palace to see the almost finished work. When he arrived, Elizabeth stepped down from the dais upon which she was posed and sent for sherry. When a footman arrived bearing a tray with only two glasses Pitman was embarrassed. It seemed Augustus was not invited to join them. The Queen smiled, sensing her visitor's perplexity, 'Mr John', she said, 'has a bottle of brandy in the cupboard. He can help himself when he wants to.'

During the 1950s the debate about representational and non-representational art continued to rage in Chelsea. Annigoni arrived to paint Elizabeth II, the new Queen, against a background which seemed distinctly 'Florentine'. The critics raved about a second Renaissance and Rose, who still rules the Launderette at Chelsea Green with a rod of iron, remembers the great artist coming in with his shirts. Annigoni is not forgotten, but David Hockney commands greater space in dictionaries of contemporary art. The distinguished horse painter, Sir Alfred Munnings, who was President of the Royal Academy but nearly expelled from the Chelsea Arts Club for reprobate behaviour, liked women to look like women. His sitters would arrive in limousines, freshly coiffured, but at his studio, Belton House in Chelsea Park Gardens, the bell push was at rider height, so that grooms could clatter down Beaufort Street and into his stable-yard.

Munnings's favourite model was his wife, Violet, who had a superb seat and knew how to sit still in a side-saddle. She appears in many of his paintings and was long considered one of Chelsea's most charming eccentrics. She had a famous Pekinese, Black Knight, and a black Labrador which accompanied her to St Andrew's Park Walk and 'sang' in unison with the choir. Lady Munnings swore the Peke gave her racing tips and so accurate were her forecasts that no one demurred. When the animal died, she had him stuffed and carried him about with her in a carpet bag.

16
Youth and Art

Alice Corbett comes of a family of artists. Her uncle, Leonard Lassalle, paints murals in the South of France and once kept an antiques shop in Tunbridge Wells, which was so esoteric, he would allow no object later than 1630 over the threshold. Her mother, Lydia Corbett, exhibits at the Francis Kyle Gallery and earned immortality at eighteen, as the model for Picasso's 'Sylvie' paintings. Alice was brought up to painting and drawing. It is in her blood. What more natural, therefore, than that when she was eighteen, she should have elected to train at Chelsea College of Art, that miscellany of departments sprawled across four far-flung sites, two of which are in Fulham and one in Shepherd's Bush.

Her father had been sometime Warden of Dartington Hall in Devon, the prestigious West Country arts centre set among acres of flower-flecked woodland. Alice was used to space, but London called and the glamour of Chelsea seemed irresistible. When she enrolled for the foundation course at Manresa Road, she was surprised by the smallness of the studios. 'Everything seemed incredibly basic and as most students couldn't afford to live in Chelsea, they were rooming where they could. I had to share a flat in Finchley. It took hours to get in every morning.'

Alice, however, was an artist of strong conviction. She didn't want to be 'just a painter' like her mother and when eventually she moved from 'Painting and Drawing' at Manresa Road to the Design Department at Hugon Road, she revelled in the three dimensional. Alice was going to be a sculptor. She had thrown off parental restraint and fallen under the spell of one of her teachers, who encouraged her to travel. 'Travel', he said, 'would enlarge the mind and increase her breadth of vision.' Florence beckoned. The thought of Michelangelo appealed to her but, as the summer vacation approached, Alice decided to set off for California to get a grip on post-Impressionism.

She reached San Francisco on the day they were opening the new Museum of Modern Art. As she queued for three hours in the blazing sunshine, Alice wondered whether she wouldn't have been better off further down the coast, lazing on a Pacific beach. But the training of Manresa Road was strong and the hype about the works of art which the new museum enshrined had been tremendous. At last the queue reached the ticket kiosk. Alice handed over her dollars. She moved into the air-conditioned building, grateful for the shade. Suddenly she gave a strangled cry. 'Maman'. The first exhibit with which she came face to face was Picasso's giant bust of 'Sylvie'. Alice gave up wanting to be a sculptor and confined herself to ceramics.

Parents did not always endorse the idea of daughters taking up sculpture with enthusiasm. Before the Second World War painting was considered more ladylike. In the early months of the War studios were still to be had in Redcliffe Road for thirty shillings a week. Chelsea College was a polytechnic and Henry Moore taught sculpture there, when Joan Wyndham went to her first Bohemian party in a cocktail dress and came back covered in dog hairs and soaked in gin. The party was given by her mother's neighbour, who announced gleefully that every walk of life would be represented, 'policemen, air-raid wardens, dukes, chars, artists, sculptors and soldiers'. At the beginning of the War it was thought rather important for a gel to become a 'good mixer'.

Joan fell in love with a particularly unwashed sculptor, who was writing a poem called 'Ecce Ego'. When her mother got her home there was a full-scale row: 'Well dear, if you like that type there are plenty to be had – they swarm in art schools, prisons, doss houses, they're laid out in rows in morgues . . . I can't understand you having such depraved taste, and I told you not to mix your drinks.'

Three months later she enrolled at the Art College. The formalities included signing some forms, paying thirty bob and being introduced to Henry Moore. She was placed in a small cell off the main studio and given a head to copy. Moore flung a lump of clay at her and told her to enjoy herself.

Innocent enjoyment was very much the key to the pre-war art world but after the War a rowdier element crept in. It found expression at the Chelsea Arts Balls, which had to be suspended after some wag let off an RAF smoke bomb at the Albert Hall. Traditionally the proceeds of the balls have gone into sustaining the members of the Chelsea Arts Club in the manner to which they have grown accustomed since 1900. The Club was founded in 1890 with Whistler and Sargent among its leading lights. It moved to its present much-loved premises a decade later – the long, low rambling house in Old Church Street with a garden at the back, filled with honeysuckle and large enough to accommodate a marquee and Orlando, the ginger tom-cat.

The first Arts Ball was held at the Royal Opera House in 1908. It was a decorous affair with tickets at half a guinea and boxes from five to eight guineas. The huge profit that year and the following year encouraged George Sherwood Foster, who was then Chairman of the Club's House Committee, to go a step further. In 1910 he grandly booked the Albert Hall. The outlay was tremendous. Sargent even offered to underwrite the event in case of financial disaster. There was no need. The ball made a profit of £1,400 and it was held annually at the Albert Hall until the outbreak of war in 1914. Before the First World War limelight was used to illuminate the dancers. Many Society beauties arrived at the 1910 ball in fabulous costumes. Mrs Rudolph Helwag came as a Sioux princess in a litter carried by real Sioux Indians bearing sharpened tomahawks. Viola Tree was a Ballad in E flat, and the fashionable novelist Arthur Alpin came plumed as a cockerel. He strutted about the dance floor crowing raucously until he collapsed with fatigue. So fine were the orange and black feathers protruding from his magnificent costume that he could not sit down. The *Illustrated London News* called the event 'the greatest fancy dress ball ever held in London, four thousand dancers on the floor of the Albert Hall.'

The early balls celebrated Mardi Gras and after the First World War Shrove Tuesday continued to be the date chosen until 1922, when it was switched to New Year's Eve. Artists and students mingled with the rich and famous, while Club stewards dressed as Beefeaters kept order. Even in the 'Roaring Twenties' there was very little trouble. One year the Prince of Wales became the Patron and Emerald Cunard and Gladys Cooper joined the committee.

Following the excitements of the Tutenkhamen expedition in 1926 an Egyptian theme was chosen. The dance floor positively seethed with Cleopatras, but the event was such a success that theme balls were held ever after. All the London art schools participated, designing outrageous floats of canvas and papier maché which were broken up by the dancers after midnight, when thousands of balloons were released from a net strung high above their heads. By 1930 a Noah's Ark theme gave rise to some undignified scuffling among the students over which animals should enter the ark first. 'Chaos at Arts Ball' screamed the next day's headlines, so the following year members of the Harlequins Rugby Club were given free tickets in exchange for their services as bouncers.

By this time the balls had become world famous and a standard fixture of the London Season. Many great artists offered to design the scenery, which was eagerly painted by students and theatre hands, thrilled to have the chance of working with a master. Augustus John participated as did the Russian scene painter, Alexander Bilibin. John, wearing a paint-stained smock, would fortify himself with sporadic tipples from a brandy bottle placed dangerously among his paint rags and jars of turpentine. The only school outside London that was ever asked to participate was the Portsmouth School of Art, whose students once produced an enormous stork with flapping wings. It flew across the hall on wires, carrying a real baby slung from its beak. The baby remained perfectly tranquil.

The dance floor positively seethed with Cleopatras . . .

Everyone alive today who attended the balls between the wars remembers them as full of colour and elegance. There was no hooliganism and certainly no nudity, although in the thirties an energetic bacchante once broke a shoulder strap in the full glare of the spotlights. Balloons were popped with hat pins. Soda siphons were squirted uproariously at starched shirts, but the bouncers seldom had to eject anyone. After the Second World War the theme was a phoenix rising resplendent from the ashes and the whole nation seemed to echo the hopefulness of Chelsea. The BBC ran a wireless programme reporting New Year celebrations through the Empire, always returning after the chimes of Big Ben to describe the breaking of the floats. Pathé News filmed the balls, rushing the spools to the cinemas to be shown on New Year's Day, while musical stars such as Jessie Matthews and Evelyn Laye came straight from the theatres to sing popular favourites.

After the war the balls gained the reputation for being rather louche. An altogether rowdier kind of merriment prevailed. When the floats were broken up, dresses were torn, jaws broken and drunken brawling set in. Booze was not cheap. Champagne had gone up to 59 shillings a bottle, while whisky and gin cost £4 10s. a bottle, roughly half a bank clerk's weekly wage, but spirits were available. At the Phoenix Ball, so festive was the atmosphere, that the Band of the Irish Guards got their orders mixed up. When called upon to remain *inside* the Hall playing 'Auld Lang Syne', they skirled out into the forecourt to the strains of an unknown Celtic air. Joseph McCulloch, a somewhat seedy member of the Arts Club, also abetted his students in preparing a float which affronted public decency.

Two nude models were tied to the stake in a scene called 'Burning Heretics', while students from Goldsmiths' College, dressed as hot little tongues of flame, flickered and writhed about their knees. The float shocked some of the female guests, who were unused to the conventions of the studio. If McCulloch had chosen languid nymphettes, or elegant showgirls, he might have got away with it, but he opted for heretics of luscious proportions, which somehow added to the obscenity. The LCC received a letter addressed to 'The Department of Public Morals'. 'At the Chelsea Arts Ball,' the writer complained, 'women were openly mixing with the throngs quite naked.' There was almost a prosecution. The press photographs were considered unprintable and Loris Rey, the Chairman of the Arts Club, suspended McCulloch from membership for three months, but when the fuss died down figure drawing became a popular pursuit.

After the Phoenix Ball stripping seemed to become an integral part of the New Year's Eve entertainment. The poet Laurie Lee remembered 'orgiastic floats sailing round the ballroom, covered in girls from banks in cheap tulle'. After midnight when the floats were ripped up, the tulle was ripped off and the slave girls plundered on red plush banquettes in the loggias. Scanty attire became vaguely associated with the whole concept of Chelsea.

By the fifties 'nice girls' were restrained from going to the balls in a last-ditch parental stand against Freud, but the battle was lost before it began. Analysis came in, closely followed by rock and roll. The rumba, a dance which was genuinely sexy, was replaced by a whole generation of rock chicks with peroxide hair. Their partners tried to emulate Elvis in the pelvic thrust. Thrusting was energetically practised up and down the King's Road for several weeks before the Arts Ball and the new music was so infectious that Nigel's unmarried aunt found herself being nudged under the table by a red-coated Chelsea Pensioner in the Kardomah Café.

17
Shoes

If you include boutiques which stock sequinned slippers and feathered flip-flops, a total of seventy-two shops sell footwear in the King's Road. Turn down the side streets and you will find more. The side streets, of course, include Old Church Street, where the King of Shoemakers, Manolo Blahnik, produces creations so erotic that some customers claim his shoes have saved their marriages. Fashion journalists never tire of pointing out that he has added a new noun to the language, 'Manolos' which is synonymous with the most luxurious footwear in the world. To own a pair confers instant status, though in Chelsea so many people do, that Manolos are simply referred to as MBs.

For real shoeaholics MBs are a cure for depression. Take out a sling-back in turquoise snake with a wickedly curved heel and a flash of provocative yellow slanted diagonally across the toe on a February morning and just to look at it banishes winter blues. This probably explains why a crocodile of jet-setting celebrities head for the premises in Old Church Street the moment they touch down at Heathrow. To put on a new pair of Manolos is regarded by many as an instant remedy against jet-lag. They revitalize the wearer. Jerry Hall, Ivana Trump and Naomi Campbell all make a bee-line for his shop, whenever their gruelling international schedules permit. Prozac would be cheaper, but not as much fun. Madonna has gone on record as placing Manolo's shoes among the best turn-ons she knows: 'Wonderful. They last longer than sex.' While Paloma Picasso, who is 'never without her Blahniks even in her dreams' lives, when in London, within walking distance of his beautiful white front door.

Although Blahnik has now 'gone global', with a store in Manhattan and mighty retail outlets in Nieman Marcus and Bergdorf Goodman, the shop in Old Church Street is still a tremendous draw. Americans, particularly, are bowled over by the bijou surroundings. No. 49, which was once the Old Dairy, stands beside Justice Walk, the quaint footpath leading into Lawrence Street. A cow's head juts from the façade and decorative tiles show a milkmaid in a perfectly stunning pink hat balancing a pail and walking across Chelsea fields to meet her sweetheart. He is a mower who can be seen leaning on his scythe contemplating a healthy flask of ale, which he has slung over the branch of a tree. To complete the rustic idyll, cattle wade in the Thames while a mallard drake conducts a brood of fluffy ducklings across the river – an early example of male parenting. By contrast, Manolo's name-plate is a masterpiece of minimalistic chic. Grey and white panels underscore the tiny vitrine in which there are rarely more than six items on display. Not a scene which you would associate with the world's movers and shakers, yet the glamorous and the super-rich flock there in droves, complaining only because there is no parking for stretch limos in Paultons Square. Even the immensely wealthy Mrs David Beckham who has recently stormed the catwalk in Ribiero's green satin football shorts, begged Manolo to design her wedding shoes. He did – silver, exclusive and televised across four continents.

Blahnik himself was born in the Canaries. The exuberant colour-sense of the islanders throbs through his collections, especially this season, when Palm Beach clothes call for strappy sandals in the hues of a really classic sunset. He and his sister Evangeline, however, are vaguely crossed with Czech blood, so that the exuberance is tempered with the old-world fastidiousness of the Austro-Hungarian Empire. 'Charmer' is always the word used of Manolo. He lives in Bath, dresses in Savile Row and was propelled into shoe design by Diana Vreeland, the legendary editor of American *Vogue* to whom he showed some drawings in 1971. By 1972 he was designing platform soles for Ossie Clark – shoes so high that Marisa Berenson and Bianca Jagger nearly fell off the catwalk. All the Jagger women adore him, but he does not aim specifically to cater for the super-rich. 'Shoes', he says, 'are entertainment, an escape. It's like Cinderella. You put them on and dream.'

Quite a lot of dreaming must go on in SW3. On sale mornings the queue outside Manolo's front door begins to form at 5 a.m. By nine o'clock it extends to the King's Road. Serious collectors sometimes need to call in a carpenter to enlarge their wardrobes, when the shoe hoard threatens to burst from the shelves. Two hundred pairs is an average number for a recognized shoeaholic. A well-dressed woman needs a shoe for every occasion.

That was certainly how Jackie Rofe felt when she fell in love with an Ambassador. He had invited her to his Belgian chateau for the week-end. She was about to step on a plane for Brussels when she realized that she had forgotten her shoes. 'Some of my greatest love affairs', recalls Jackie 'have begun with a pair of MBs. No self-respecting woman should start an adventure without a sable and a good pair of shoes.' Dressed in a deep blue Missoni suit and with no time even to pop into Gina of Sloane Street for the missing accessories, she borrowed a pair from her friend Jackie Palmer, who sells antique silver at Antiquarius – brand new Manolos in midnight blue suede. When Mrs Rofe reached the château, there was dew on the grass. Terrified of ruining her friend's costly treasures, she reacted accordingly.

'Why are you taking your shoes off?' asked the bewildered diplomat.

'I love the feel of wet grass,' she lied. 'It's so romantic.'

The shoes remained intact but, happily, Mrs Rofe did not. She put them on again at the bedroom door, when she had dried her soaking feet on the acres of Aubusson carpet.

The connection between shoes and romance goes back into the mists of time. No one who saw Luis Buñuel's film *Diary of a Chambermaid* can forget the scene when Jeanne Moreau, her ankles encased in high, buttoned boots, leans back and allows the soft leather to be caressed by her fetishist employer. Anyone intrigued by the history of shoes should also drop in at Blue Velvet, where Frederick's collection of shoe pictures decorates the walls from floor to ceiling. Frederick – he never uses a surname – has traded in the King's Road for over twenty years, designing and manufacturing his own range: ponyskin boots, glacé calf courts and diamanté evening sandals, very modestly priced at about £110. The smoky topaz are to die for, being the perfect accompaniment to taupe, which is in again, and flaunted shamelessly all over Brompton Cross, where Joseph has declared it the only chic alternative to fuchsia.

Frederick bought the shoe pictures from the Frankfurt Museum many years ago, when he was in the dress business. Shoes, he insists, are only his hobby, but the elegant pictures in their walnut frames have become his hallmark. To the customer who has gone in for a pair of sale-price tiger-print mules, they are also an education. Curvaceous button boots, scarlet- and gold-laced as worn in Vienna in 1910, vie for attention with foot-high pattens, the 'shoes on stilts' favoured by a Venetian courtesan *c*. 1575 to keep her skirts out of the mud. Flip-flops, it seems, were known to the Romans, while the square-toed Tudors with their disgraceful passion for slashed brocade were shoeaholic beyond belief.

Owing to the high business rates, retailers will tell you that only chain stores can now survive in the section of King's Road between Sloane Square and Oakley Street. This means that shoe giants like Bally, which is globally backed, or the cheaply cheerful Dune of Oxford Street can trade alongside Next and FCUK, and Marks & Spencer, but for boutiques the cost is prohibitive, so that the small individual shops for which Chelsea is so famous have mostly been pushed to the lower end of the road, where rates are not as high.

A happy exception is R. Soles, the provocatively named boot suppliers opposite the Pheasantry. Judy and Paul quite simply have a big enough turnover to defy the business rates. Women come from the fashion capitals of the world to buy their cowboy boots and western accessories. Judy Rothschild has been with the store almost since it began but, a few years ago, finding the shoe companies 'totally boring', she redesigned the whole collection. Celebrity customers flock to Judy and Paul. Supermodels and rock chicks are among their clientèle, as well as our home-bred 'It' girls, Tara Palmer-Tomkinson and Tamara Beckwith. A few months ago Tara coveted purple python couture boots and cheerfully announced in her *Sunday Times* 'Yah' column that she would 'work in a plague pit' to earn them. She was talking made-to-measure from Gina of Sloane Street, of course. Several weeks later the *Daily Mail*'s intrepid profile writer Lynda Lee-Potter revealed that Tara turned up at the Berkeley Hotel in the purple boots, adding rather unkindly that the 'It' girl gets discount. Jealousy is so unbecoming. Judy and Paul do the python boots in fuschia and also in glorious rainbow-coloured snakeskin. At £385 a pair they slightly undercut Manolo, but it takes a lot of chutzpah to wander into the Goat in Boots with a carrier bag emblazoned 'R. Soles'.

18

Organically Yours

In a shop called Rococo at the bottom of the King's Road, Chantal Coady sells delicious organic chocolate. She has written a book full of fascinating facts about cocoa, which the Aztecs called food of the Gods. She considers the eighteenth century was the supremely elegant age of chocolate consumption. Chantal has decorated her shop in a pretty style which recalls the heyday of Ranelagh Gardens, when Mozart, a child prodigy of eight and a half, played the harpsichord at a charity concert in the Rotunda. He stayed in Chelsea and probably sampled the delights of the famous Bun House, where even the children of George II and George III went to eat Chelsea Buns, those lavish coils of sweetened pastry, stuffed with currants and iced with sugar. Inevitably, the infant George IV was hyperactive.

Chantal's own chocolate kitchen is in Vauxhall on the site of the earlier pleasure gardens, but everything about her shop evokes the more refined atmosphere of Ranelagh, where Horace Walpole was to be seen nightly in his lavender-coloured dress coat. Pictures of the plants used medicinally by Sir Hans Sloane decorate the walls of Rococo and even the chocolate bars are in blue and white wrappers, printed with eighteenth-century chocolate moulds in the shapes of birds and butterflies. 'Chocolate', Chantal says, 'was almost certainly drunk in Don Saltero's Coffee House in Cheyne Walk, although it would have cost twice the price of coffee.' At the Rotunda, where the brilliant lights used for balls and masquerades made everyone exclaim that it was like a fairy palace, the luxurious drink would have been prepared over open fires which, rather surprisingly, burned inside the great wooden dome, as well as outside in the pleasure gardens. Its delicate aromas must have wafted deliciously on the breeze, for our ancestors mixed it with costly perfumes like rose petals or frankincense. At Rococo they sell bars flavoured with orange and geranium, wild mint, nutmeg, rosemary or cardamom.

Chocolate was drunk in England from the middle of the seventeenth century. Its early uses were distinctly medicinal. Pepys used it as a cure for his hangover the morning after Charles II's coronation, but Sir Hans Sloane was the first person to add milk to it. Before his innovation the drinking chocolate served at the Cocoa Tree in Pall Mall and White's Chocolate House in St James's was a dark liquid made by pouring boiling water onto grated chocolate. The result was that an oily scum formed and floated evilly to the top. The French beat it out with a chocolate stick, or molina. In France great ladies had their own chocolate maids, whose specific duty was to prepare the beverage. In Mozart's *Così Fan Tutte*, Despina complains, 'I've been beating chocolate for half an hour.'

Modern research shows that unrefined chocolate contains theobromine, a stimulant like the caffeine in coffee or theine in tea, which activates brain and muscle performance. It is only when it is mixed with too much sugar that it is responsible for tooth decay, migraine and obesity. For many years cocoa was officially provided by the Royal Navy for sailors on night watch. Recent findings have prompted some homoeopathic doctors to prescribe chocolate bars as an alternative to St John's Wort, the Prozac of the organically eating classes, although it is scarcely less addictive. The most reasonably priced drinking chocolate on offer in SW3 is 'finest Suchard' at £1.50 in Daisy and Tom, the children's alternative to the Bluebird Gastrodome.

Health Food abounds in Chelsea in many unexpected varieties. Directly opposite the Gastrodome with its lovingly culled organic rocket, New Culture Revolution, the Chinese restaurant with pale yellow walls, minimalist tables and free postcards for those who wish to communicate without e-mail, advertises 'healthy eating for every day'. It serves noodles and dumplings at student prices, laced liberally with nutritious seaweed, raw salmon, or 'Fried Prawns Fisherman's Style'. The menu carols the virtues of Jiao ji main, the staple diet of Northern China, where the cold, tough climate, so like our own, means food must be served in robust and generous portions. 'No Monosodium Glutamate' proclaims the menu, but for those who want to live dangerously, soy sauce is available in discreet white jugs. It is not a place to lunch with wheat-allergic girl friends, who prefer to nibble nervously at a Holland & Barrett rice cake, or the candida-conscious who might blench at the yeasty Tsing tao beer.

One of the earliest organic restaurants began back in the 1970s when everyone was walking about the King's Road in boots from the Chelsea Cobbler, dyed red and green straight out of a jewel-bright LSD reverie. A girl called Sue started the Flying Dragon Café. It was lit by candles and silk-embroidered cushions replaced chairs. It smelled of sandalwood, served seven kinds of tea, yoghurt with honey and bread made from stoneground floor. Hashish was freely consumed. By the eighties the Farmer's Market became the green nerve centre. It was established in Sydney Street on land leased by the Royal Brompton Hospital. The market was intended to be a temporary fixture until the Hospital decided how to develop the site. Shops were set up in charming wooden chalets. Fresh produce included grouse from Lord Lambton's estate, herbs growing in pots and fish from the Abinger Trout Farm.

Jack Beanstalk, the forerunner of the Chelsea Gardener, had a Frog Island Fish Farm at the back where live trout swam about in a pond. Neal's Yard opened premises and still have one chalet selling herbal teas and their aromatherapy range in the distinctive blue bottles. Nostalgia reigned. Anyone who could not get to the country at the weekend headed for Sydney Street to queue for hours to buy 'decent bread' or stoneground flour. Baguette sales went into decline and white sugar was banned from the progressive tea-table. I even remember my otherwise sane mother-in-law hissing 'Poison' when she saw me proffer

Tate & Lyle's sugar cubes to a conventionally bred Irish dowager who lived in Sloane Street.

The Farmer's Market went from strength to strength, but in 1990 the Hospital decided it was time to develop the site. The decision split the Chelsea Society. Lord Cadogan and the Vice Chairman, the actress Felicity Kendal, were up in arms when the 'charming chalets' were referred to as 'a bit of a shanty town' by the Society's Chairman, David Le Lay. The Hospital, however, had 'royal immunity' to develop as it pleased. By 1995 Lady Wynne-Jones and the friends of Chelsea brought in the light artillery. Peter Townend, the Social Editor of *Tatler*, one of Chelsea's most influential figures, because he orchestrates the Deb. Season, joined the fray. Nobody is entirely clear what happened next. The Chelsea Library has a dearth of cuttings on the subject and St James's Palace is maintaining a discreet silence, but it is said that at the mention of the word 'organic' there was a letter from You Know Whom.

The Farmer's Market continues to thrive. You can no longer buy organic bread there, for that you must go to Chelsea Green, but on Saturday mornings the chalets are as busy as ever and very much a family scene. At Cheeky Boo, the wooden hut with a walk-in humidor, you can buy Toscani cheroots, as smoked by Clint Eastwood in the spaghetti Westerns, or an Al Capone-sized Monte Cristo cigar. Americans adore the place. They can buy Cuban tobacco there without paying the high tax charged in the USA. The place is always full of macho men ignoring government health warnings. Naturally this lures the more discerning breed of Chelsea Chick. Charles Conway, the manager, is instructing his Saturday staff, in this case a beautiful brunette in her first year at King's College, London. She is called Arethusa and has lived in Chelsea all her life.

Over at the Market Place Restaurant they are topping up the cappuccinos in huge white cups. A stunning pair of Chicks swing in, bearing Blue Velvet bags. They have had a shoe binge chez Frederick. One of them wears a diamond-studded millennium cross from Theo Fennel the jeweller who is the grown up's version of the Non-Stop Party Shop. The other pulls a little packet from V.V. Rouleaux out of a Gucci bag. She has bought braid to up-date her jeans. In La Pizzeria they are sizzling the Margheritas and a couple of Spanish au pairs have just emerged with a trio of under-tens from the Non-Stop Party Shop. The children want to go to Daisy and Tom to watch the marionettes, but the Spanish girls would like to go to El Gaucho. Perhaps it is for the tortillas, or perhaps it is because a famous Formula One driver has just walked across to the other side of the square. For this is Chelsea. This is Celebrityville.

Charles comes out of his humidor with two long-haired dachshunds on leads. One is Cheeky, after whom the cigar shop is named. At the Market Place Restaurant, Terry, the manager, is a bit stressed. He has just read that the hospital needs two hundred million pounds for its new development. It seems the Market is under threat again. The Sydney Street site is 'worth a packet'. Someone mentions Chelsea's richest philanthropist, Vivien Duffield. She has just saved the Royal Opera House and given a wing to the Tate. Perhaps she will save the Farmer's Market too. Vivian lives near the river at a meritorious address. She is invoked as regularly as St Thomas More. Charles Conway points to the sign which says 'Organic Warehouse Coming Soon'. He smiles a nice, slow, phlegmatic, English smile. 'This is Chelsea,' he says. 'Whatever happens, we won't give in without a fight.'